MODERN ECONOMIC ISSUES

OTTO ECKSTEIN, Harvard University, General Editor

In this series the great public issues in economics are posed and put in perspective by original commentary and reprints of the most interesting and significant recent statements by experts in economics and government.

BENJAMIN CHINITZ, the editor of this volume, is Chairman of the Department of Economics and Associate Director of the Center for Regional Economic Studies at the University of Pittsburgh. After receiving his doctorate from Harvard University, he taught at Dartmouth College and Brown University and served as a consultant to the Connecticut State Development Commission, the RAND Corporation, and the President's Appalachian Regional Commission. Dr. Chinitz is author of *Freight and the Metropolis* and co-author of *Projection of a Metropolis* and *Region in Transition* (Volume I of the Pittsburgh Regional Economic Study).

CITY AND SUBURB

The Economics of
Metropolitan Growth

CITY AND SUBURB

THE ECONOMICS OF METROPOLITAN GROWTH

Edited by Benjamin Chinitz

A SPECTRUM BOOK

PRENTICE-HALL, Inc., Englewood Cliffs, N.J.

CONTENTS

CITY AND SUBURB

The Economics of
Metropolitan Growth

INTRODUCTION

CITY AND SUBURB

Benjamin Chinitz

Americans have been moving to urban areas almost from the word *go*. They have been leaving the farm where 90 per cent of them used to earn their livelihood back in 1780 and have been settling in cities and the surrounding suburbs. Today, 70 per cent of them reside in urban areas.

In the nineteenth century, this great migration might have been characterized in terms of *rural* and *urban*. In the twentieth century it has taken on a new dimension—not just urban, but *metropolitan*. The metropolitan area received formal official recognition in the census of 1940—in which 140 areas, accounting for 48 per cent of the population, were defined as *metropolitan*. Such areas now account for 63 per cent of the nation's population. The trend toward metropolitan living is strong and observers are unanimous in projecting the trend into the future. It is expected, for example, that 75 per cent of the population will be living in such areas by 1985—although they will probably have a new name at that time.

How does *metropolitan* differ from *urban*? *Urban* implies high-density spatial arrangements—a lot of people and a lot of business clustered into a small area (small, that is, by comparison to national averages). In the United States as a whole, for example, the average square mile claims 50 inhabitants; but in New York State it claims 350 and in New York City, 4,977!

Densities vary within New York City—they are at their highest in Manhattan and lowest in Staten Island. But all of New York City is under one political roof—or to put it more exactly, there is at least one political body whose jurisdiction is coincident with the boundaries of New York City: the government of the City of New York. So far, so urban. We "go metropolitan" when we face this fact of life: just outside the borders of this great city and other cities there are contiguous areas of relatively high density—that is, "high"

3

relative to the rural pattern, though low relative to the big-city
pattern. In other words there are urban-like areas, *under separate
political* jurisdictions right next door to the big city. There is a lot
of interaction between the central city and the surrounding areas;
people telephone, shop, commute to work, and travel for weekend
recreation—all of which generates a lot of trespassing by political
neighbors on each other's properties. If the central city has a population of 50,000 and the outside community meets some very simple
standards of urbanism and connection to the center, then we have
—by 1960 standards—a *standard metropolitan statistical area.* In
other words, we have a metropolitan area—an area in which many
urban communities are located in close proximity to one another.

How much is *many?* The census gobbles up surrounding areas to
form metropolitan areas by adding counties—i.e., it is the county as
a unit which is subjected to the dual tests of urbanity and connection to the center. But to judge by counties is to underestimate
vastly the political jungle which characterizes most metropolitan
areas. There are literally hundreds of separate jurisdictions in most
of the large metropolitan areas. Before we enter this maze to see
what special economic problems it poses to modern society, we
must consider the fundamental economic forces which are pushing
us into this pattern of living.

THE MOVEMENT INTO METROPOLITAN AREAS

What lies behind the rapid and accelerating growth of metropolitan areas in the United States? Why is a larger and larger
proportion of the nation's growing population choosing to live and
work within the confines of the metropolitan complexes which cover
a relatively minuscule portion of the nation's total area? The answer
lies partly in the changes in patterns of production. Over the past
century there have been drastic shifts in the kinds of goods which
society wants and in the inputs which are required to produce them
efficiently. But there have been shifts in consumption patterns as
well, as more and more Americans achieve both the income with
which to afford the good things in life and the leisure in which to
enjoy them. And many of the refinements of twentieth-century

living are most easily acquired—and often best enjoyed—in proximity to a fairly large number of other people with similar tastes and demands.

Push and Pull

One of the most obvious effects of industrialization and economic progress has been a steady drop in the extent to which people live directly off the land. For many decades the proportion of Americans employed in agriculture, mining, fishing, forestry, and the other "primary" industries whose products are the fruits of nature more or less in their original state has been declining sharply—from 40 per cent of the total work force employed at the turn of the century to only 10 per cent in 1960. This is in part because the demand for the products of primary industries has not nearly kept pace with the long-term growth of income and consumption in the United States. When people find themselves twice as rich as they were before, they do not generally—at least in this country—eat twice as much or use twice as much cloth to cover themselves. Rather, they tend to expend their increased wealth on higher-quality goods and even more on different types of consumption which cannot be satisfied by the products of farm or forest, of sea or mine. They tend to spend a larger and larger share of their income on cars and entertainment, on education for their children and medical care for their families—goods which are either the end product of a long and complicated fabrication process or which are not really tangible "goods" at all.

Not only is the demand for the products of the land-bound primary industries steadily decreasing in proportion to the total demand for goods and services in the United States, but the number of man-hours required to produce any given quantity of these primary products has been dropping sharply and persistently. Since 1947, American labor productivity in agriculture and mining has more than doubled—an increase more rapid than that which has characterized most manufacturing industries and much more rapid than that experienced in the growing service sectors. In sum, the direct fruits of the land represent a shrinking portion of the population's total consumption of goods and services, and every year fewer people are required to satisfy each unit of demand that remains.

With the decline of agriculture and the extractive industries, which together have always formed the economic backbone of rural and small-town life, it is not surprising that more and more people should move into the cities and their surrounding areas. Man is a social animal: he desires privacy but he generally desires companionship more. As technological process enables more and more people to earn their living within smaller and smaller areas, their reaction is to move closer to their fellow men and to the goods and services which are available in full variety only to a large, compact market. In general, it is the metropolitan areas which can best provide these while offering, at the same time, a choice of urban, suburban, or rural living within their boundaries.

If the decline in the importance of primary industries has provided the push toward metropolitan areas, the pull has come from the increasing importance of other industries. The fastest-growing segment of the economy in recent years has been that vast complex of functions generally lumped together as the "service" or "tertiary" sector. This area of American economic life includes trade and distribution activities, such business services as finance, advertising, research, and central office administration, and an enormous variety of personal services, of which education, medical care, repair services, and entertainment represent only a small part. The reasons for the rapid growth of employment in these industries (which has averaged 3 per cent annually since 1947 as compared with an annual growth rate of 1 per cent for employment in the nation as a whole) reflect those already advanced for the decline of agriculture and the extractive industries. More and more of the income of the American people is spent on the services provided by these industries. At the same time, these industries have so far been those least affected by technological progress; labor productivity has increased far less rapidly in the service industries than in either agriculture or manufacturing, so that the share of national employment accounted for by the services sector has risen even more than the share of national output accounted for by its "products."

Production Trends

The kinds of labor or skills required for the production of services are very different from those required in farming or mining. The changed requirements have, in general, a strong urban bias. The need for physical strength and manual dexterity has been almost entirely replaced by the need for a high level of literacy, for professional and technical knowledge, for clerical skills, for the kind of sophistication that allows ease and familiarity in the handling of complicated processes and large bodies of information. And people with the kind of background, education, and inclinations to encourage the development of these attributes are generally to be found in cities—and in greatest supply in the large cities which form the core of metropolitan areas. For those service industries which require a large female clerical force (with its characteristically high turnover rate as girls leave their jobs to marry and have babies), only a metropolitan area can provide a large enough pool of potential workers within easy commuting distance. In addition, the metropolitan area, with its close-linked, far-reaching network of utilities and services, offers access to a large supply of technical and office skills while allowing the employer to choose between an urban location in the center and a suburban one nearer the periphery.

For manufacturing, the third major sector of the American economy (and until very recently the largest), the situation is more complicated and the relationship to increasing metropolitanization less clear-cut. The trend seems to be toward decentralization of manufacturing activity. During much of this century manufacturing employment has tended to spread out and away from its historical concentration in the large urban centers, and the share of the nation's manufacturing jobs accounted for by large metropolitan areas seems to have declined slightly.

The chief cause of this dispersion of activity has unquestionably been the development of new modes of transportation. In the days when rail and waterways were the most efficient means of moving both people and goods from one place to another, it was not only natural but essential for manufacturing activity to cluster in the large cities which grew up at the nodal points of these transport systems. With the advent of the automobile and the truck and the development of an increasingly widespread network of roads to carry them, this situation changed rapidly. Freed from their dependence on fixed lines of transportation, manufacturers were able to consider other factors in choosing their locations, and in many cases these other considerations led them out of the great urban centers into the nonmetropolitan parts of the country.

By mid-century, however, the decentralizing effect of the truck and the automobile had been largely spent, and a variety of forces operating in favor of a new metropolitan concentration came to the fore. Some of these forces consist of still newer developments in transportation which tend to restore the historical advantage of the metropolitan area. The advent of jet transport is one such development; another is the increasing importance of piggyback transport (the carrying of truck trailers on specially designed railroad flat cars). These new transport modes have acted as brakes on decentralization because the expense of constructing a modern jet airport, or of maintaining the complex and expensive terminal facilities required for efficient piggyback operations, can be supported only by the concentration of people and the large markets found in metropolitan areas.

Other forces are also at work to halt the dispersion of manufacturing activity. One important factor is the steadily decreasing dependence of manufacturing on specific raw material inputs. The importance of raw materials in the manufacturing process has been lessening for a number of reasons—one of which is industrial advancement itself. Manufactured goods are subjected to a constantly increasing amount of processing. The natural fruits of the earth pass through ever more numerous and ever more complex operations before they reach their final form: iron is turned into steel of a hundred different qualities and characteristics before it is made into cars or machines or instruments; wood is converted into paper or cardboard and then turned into hundreds of kinds of boxes and containers. The effect of all this processing is, of course, to reduce the role played by raw material costs in the total cost of the finished product.

The resource inputs required in the manufacturing process are not only becoming less important, relatively, but they are also becoming more and more diversified. The tendency of technological progress during this century seems to have been, on balance, to reduce the dependence of a manufacturing process on any particular raw material. A hundred years ago, the quality of steel and the cost of its production were both heavily dependent on the quality of the coal and of the pig iron available for making it; today low-grade coal or other fuels can be utilized just about as well, and scrap iron can be used along with pig iron without any sacrifice of quality. The creation of a vast pipeline network has sharply reduced the energy-cost disadvantages suffered by producers far from petroleum and natural gas supplies; the advent of slurry pipelines may do the same for coal-users in the near future. More and more, advances in technology are enabling men to make use of nature's most plentiful and ubiquitous resources—air, water (and soon, perhaps), solar heat—both as energy sources and as the basic ingredients for some of the manmade materials which are in many cases replacing natural raw materials in the manufacturing process.

As technology has reduced the dependence of manufacturing on raw materials, it has increased the dependence of one manufacturing operation on another. As the chain of fabrication and assembly has grown longer and more complex, the outputs of a number of manufacturing industries—of the chemicals and metals industries, for example—have increasingly become the inputs of others. This increased specialization leads to an increased interdependence among various types of manufacturing establishments. Manufacturers of intermediate or producer goods must be close to industrial markets of sufficient size to support their large-scale operations— close, that is, to a large cluster of other manufacturing firms. Producers of final goods must have easy access both to the intermediate goods needed as inputs and to the markets for the final product. In these terms, the solution for both groups is the same: to cluster close to one another within the large metropolitan areas which alone can provide both inputs and markets in sufficient scale and variety to meet their total needs.

All in all, then, the forces pulling manufacturing employment into the metropolitan areas seem to be increasing rather than diminishing in strength. This is not to deny, of course, that there are also forces at work in the opposite direction. One of these centrifugal forces is the difference in labor costs between metropolitan and nonmetropolitan areas. Although certain manufacturing industries depend heavily on the low-wage labor culled from the new immigrant and other disadvantaged minority groups congregated in some of the largest cities—the reliance of the New York garment industry on low-wage Puerto Rican labor is an example—the fact remains that wages are typically higher in the nation's metropolitan centers than in smaller urban or nonurban locations. There are several reasons for this pattern: labor unions tend to be better organized in the big cities and their bargaining strength therefore greater there than elsewhere; living costs are typically lower outside the boundaries of metropolitan areas; and the steady decrease in agricultural and mining jobs feeds an excess labor supply in rural areas and small towns which exerts a continuous downward pressure on wages in such areas. Similarly, there are often differentials in space costs between metropolitan and nonmetropolitan areas. Although a metropolitan complex typically includes suburban and even rural locations, space shortages do arise as the complex grows, and firms with particular space requirements may find that these needs can be satisfied more readily, or at lower cost, beyond metropolitan boundaries.

Consumption Trends

So far, there have been a number of shifts in the pattern of production in the United States which may help to explain why a growing proportion of the nation's jobs are to be found in metropolitan areas. But the picture is not complete without some mention of the shifts in tastes and technology which make the metropolitan area an increasingly desirable place in which to *live* as well as to *work*. We have already mentioned some of the reasons why services, which occupy an increasingly large portion of American consumer demand, are best produced in a metropolitan setting. But since services are characteristically difficult to transport from one place to another, they are best consumed in a metropolitan setting as well. Institutions of higher education, highly specialized medical or legal facilities, theaters, symphonies, and nightclubs—it is on such things that more and more of America's growing wealth is being spent, and they are available in greatest abundance within metropolitan areas.

Although the advantage of metropolitan areas is greatest in the provision of highly specialized services, recent advances in technology seem to be creating a tendency for their advantage to increase in the consumption of certain tangible goods as well. This was not always so; the most important innovations made available to the consumer during the first half of this century—electricity, the radio, the automobile, the movies, television—all tended to reduce the disadvantages of living outside of metropolitan areas, to make more and more of the niceties enjoyed by the city-dweller available to his rural neighbor as well. But today, the complexity and vast expense of many of the items demanded by both individuals and business firms may once again be widening the gap between metropolitan and nonmetropolitan living. For instance, as we have already pointed out, it takes a metropolitan area to support a jet airport, although the same is not true of the smaller facilities required to service propeller aircraft. In the days when almost all the medical equipment available could fit into the doctor's black bag, the sick man in a rural farmhouse was just as likely to be cured as the one in the big city; today much of the lifesaving equipment which scientific advances have made available is so complex and expensive that only the largest hospitals can afford it. Similarly, almost any businessman anywhere can afford a desk calculator, but it is generally in metropolitan areas that one finds the great computer complexes whose services an increasing number of firms desire but only the largest can afford to provide for themselves.

What do all these changes portend for the future growth of metropolitan areas? In the production sector, the forces of attraction and repulsion will doubtless continue to work against each other. By now the effect of the decline in agricultural and mining employment is largely spent, simply because there are few jobs left in these industries; but the expansion of jobs in the service industries, and particularly such business services as data-processing and research, will continue and perhaps accelerate. For the manufacturing sector, some new developments—such as the availability of atomic power for industrial use—are likely to continue the process of emancipation from sources of raw materials and increase the attractions of metropolitan locations. Other changes—such as developments in the manufacture of steel which serve to reduce the scale required for efficient production—are likely to operate in the direction of decentralization. As more and more manufacturing workers exchange their blue collars for white ones, the attractions of an urban labor force will grow, but these advantages could be nullified if space, labor, and other costs of doing business increase disproportionately as part of the growing pains of metropolitan areas.

In consumption trends, too, the future is far from clear. It is certain that the demand for complex and expensive goods and sophisticated services—items best consumed in a metropolitan setting—will continue to grow faster than the demand for goods and services as a whole. But as people get richer and transportation more rapid, more people will be able to live where they please and spend their money where they can get what they want.

Which set of forces will prove the stronger, the centripetal or the centrifugal? The signs suggest that the trends which have prevailed throughout this century will continue, that a larger and larger share of the nation's population will live and work within metropolitan areas. Whether such areas grow faster or more slowly than the nation as a whole, there is no question that they are going to grow or that this growth will engender new benefits and opportunities, new challenges and difficulties. The manner in which the benefits and opportunities are utilized and the challenges and difficulties met and overcome will play a large role in determining the quality of life in our country.

THE STRUCTURE OF THE METROPOLITAN ECONOMY

So far, we have talked about metropolitan areas as if they were all the same, as alike as bottles of homogenized milk. Actually, they come in an assortment more varied than the wines of France, often with nothing more in common than conformity to the minimum standards of size and density set by the Bureau of the Census. They range in size all the way from greater New York's more than 10 million inhabitants down to the 65,000 people who together form the Standard Metropolitan Statistical Area of San Angelo, Texas. Some of these metropolitan areas were great urban centers even before the nation was born; others earned the title only in 1960. Some, like New York and San Francisco, are great trading, financial, and cultural centers as well as the homes of an enormous variety of manufacturing establishments whose products are marketed throughout the country. Others, like Pittsburgh and Detroit, have grown up largely as one-industry towns, heavily committed to the production of a single commodity or of closely related groups of commodities and generally with relatively little involvement in the "nonproductive" business and consumer service or distribution activities which have come to be regarded as metropolitan specialties.

The *raison d'être* of any metropolitan area is specialization and trade with the outside world. And because any area's structure and development are very closely tied up with the kinds of specialties it offers in trade, it is both customary and convenient to divide the metropolitan economy into two parts: those industries directed toward other markets and those directed chiefly toward the local market. These two fundamental divisions are often termed the *basic* and *local-market oriented* sectors, respectively.

Basic Industries

It is by its pattern of specialization, its export or basic industries, that a metropolitan area is most easily characterized, and it is in this segment of the economy that the different areas exhibit the widest diversity. Some of the areas developed because their natural resource endowments or their strategic locations gave them a distinct advantage in one or two industries. Some have remained closely associated with these traditional specialties ever since (as, for example, Pittsburgh with steel, Akron with rubber, Omaha with meat-processing, Minneapolis with flour-milling), although those areas which have continued to grow and thrive in the mid-twentieth century have all broadened their original export base to include a variety of new specialties as well. Others acquired their major specialties almost by accident, as Detroit acquired the automobile industry, and then built up a real advantage in those lines of production through what may be loosely termed the economies of agglomeration. Some metropolitan areas specialize in the large-scale heavy manufacturing industries whose customers are mainly other industries, while others concentrate on consumer products. And some, including nearly all of the greatest metropolitan giants, specialize in a great variety of industries, large-scale and small-scale, exporting both producer goods and consumer goods. The New York metropolitan area, for example, accounts for more than 30 per cent of the nation's total employment in nearly one hundred of the nation's 446 manufacturing industries. It is beyond the scope of this discussion to list all the goods New York exports to the markets of the nation, but many have certain things in common: they tend to be consumer goods, of high value in relation to their weight or bulk, and highly unstandardized (that is, subject to frequent and drastic changes). The nation's other great metropolises—Chicago, Los Angeles, and Philadelphia, for example—also produce several hundred different types of manufactured goods and, although they do not export all or even most of them to other areas, each one possesses a long and varied list of export specialties.

All metropolitan areas have in common their heavy dependence on trade and specialization, but it is a dependence at a very different level, and in a very different sense, from that of a farm or small town which sells a single product and relies on the outside world to provide it with nearly all the other necessities of life. For another common characteristic of metropolitan areas is their very high degree of economic self-sufficiency. No metropolitan area produces everything it consumes, of course, and trade must involve imports as well as exports, but most metropolitan areas are capable of providing for a large proportion of their own needs. In making this assertion, we must remember the difference between a city and a metropolitan area. Cut off from the outside world, New York City would starve to death in short order, but the New York metropolitan area might survive a little longer, although it would find its diet painfully restricted. For the New York metropolitan area includes not only the city and its bedrooms, but also the truck and potato farms of Suffolk County and the dairy farms of outer Westchester. The same variety of land use is characteristic of nearly all of the nation's metropolitan areas.

Local-Market Industries

Metropolitan areas are more alike in the goods they produce for local consumption than in those they produce for export. This is because there are certain types of goods which consumers everywhere demand and which are easily or feasibly transported over long distances—dairy products and most fresh foods are one example, newspapers are another—and it is these goods which nearly every metropolitan area produces for itself. Areas vary tremendously, of course, in the breadth of their production for local consumption—the largest metropolitan areas tend to produce some of almost every type of manufactured good (many of them largely for local consumption), while the smaller ones must rely on a wider variety of imports. And a particular area's exports naturally help to determine the things which it makes for its own use as well. But it is possible to classify certain industries or products as generally local-market oriented, and almost every metropolitan area is engaged to a greater or lesser extent in the production of such goods.

It is above all the production of nontangible services that characterizes the self-sufficiency of metropolitan areas. We have already explained some of the reasons for which many business and consumer services are best produced in a metropolitan setting. Many are, by their nature, difficult to export. Some can, of course, be exported in indirect ways: a metropolitan area can serve as a wholesaling or financial center for the surrounding region or even, as with New York's Wall Street or Hartford's insurance complex, for the entire nation. People come into the metropolitan area to take advantage of almost any of its services and then go home again; sometimes they even stay home and simply send their problem, be it a delicate machine in need of repair or a question on financial reorganization. But the fact remains that it is largely for their own consumption that metropolitan areas generate the vast complex of services which gives all such areas, however diverse their underlying structures, a common look, and distinguishes them from the non-metropolitan parts of the nation.

Once started, this process tends to feed upon its own growth. This is partly because metropolitan-dwellers tend to have a greater demand for services and higher incomes with which to satisfy these demands than does the population at large. But it is also partly a function of the difficulties or "diseconomies" inevitably associated with metropolitan living—difficulties which require an increased number and variety of people to be offset. It takes a good many more middlemen, for example, to get a fresh egg to a housewife in midtown Manhattan than to one in a small town or rural area. Similarly, it requires more laundries, policemen, window-washers, and government clerks to maintain the customary American standards of individual cleanliness, comfort, convenience, and safety in a metropolitan setting.

VARIATIONS IN GROWTH RATES

Metropolitan areas as a whole are expanding—not only in absolute size, but also in the proportion of the nation's people and jobs encompassed within their borders. As has been noted, despite their great variety of export production patterns, all—or almost all—metropolitan areas have certain things in common: a high degree of self-sufficiency in providing the goods and services required by their own markets and, most particularly, a heavy involvement in a particular set of highly specialized and refined service activities. But despite this vigorous over-all growth and the similarities which stamp metropolitan economies, the growth experiences of individual metropolitan areas have varied enormously. During the most recent decade some, like Phoenix, Arizona, have doubled in size; others, like Pittsburgh and Boston, have remained almost at a standstill; a very few—Jersey City, for example—have actually lost ground.

What has caused some metropolitan areas to grow at an explosive rate and others not to grow at all? There are a few very simple answers—factors which help to explain the diversity of growth experience but which by no means represent the whole story nor even the major part of it. One of these factors is geographical location. Like people, metropolitan areas tend to grow faster when they are young; thus those areas located in the newer, more recently settled and industrialized parts of the country are in general growing faster than those in the long-established parts of the nation. In general, such areas have grown faster in the West than in the East, faster in the South than in the North, fastest of all in the Southwest and slowest of all in the Northeast.

Size is another of the simple factors which seems to play a role in the rate of growth. In general—and with some outstanding exceptions, such as Los Angeles—the nation's largest metropolitan areas have not been growing as fast as some of the smaller ones. An examination of the pressures which arise to impede metropolitan growth will reveal why rapid expansion should come more easily to a small or middle-sized metropolitan area than to a giant one.

Such factors as location and size are actually only a partial explanation of the differences in growth. In every region of the country and in every size category there are metropolitan areas which have been enjoying vigorous growth and others whose growth had been sickly or nonexistent. Other, more subtle factors are involved —some of them related to observable differences in the structure of the metropolitan economy (in the employment "mix" or industry "mix" of one area as opposed to that of another) and others to intangible differences in the ability to adjust to shifts both in consumer demand and in the competitive advantages possessed by a particular area or region to satisfy some part of the total demand.

The Direct Influence of "Mix"

To begin with, an area's population and employment are more likely to grow rapidly if the export activities which underlie its economic structure are concentrated in fast-growing rather than slow-growing industries. For an industry to be fast-growing in terms of employment, two things are required: total demand for its output must be expanding vigorously, and labor productivity in that particular line must not be rising so fast as to prevent a growth of output from being translated into employment growth as well. An area specialized in the aircraft industry, for instance, which has been fast-growing on both counts during the postwar era, would be expected to exhibit a higher rate of over-all growth than another heavily committed, say, to coal-mining, an industry in which slackening demand and rapidly rising labor productivity have combined to produce a rapid nationwide drop in employment.

A fast-growing mix of industries will not insure an area's growth, however, if competitive shifts cause a shrink in its share of the industries in which it is specialized. This question of industry share is closely related both to size and to geographical location. The population and income of the United States, once heavily concentrated in the nation's northeastern quadrant, have been steadily spreading out more evenly over the nation as a whole. At the same time, a number of technological changes have combined to make many manufacturing industries more closely market-oriented than ever before. As a result, many of the older and larger industrial centers, particularly in the Northeast, are finding that their traditional industrial specialties, areas in which they once dominated national production, are following the markets across the country, either through the relocation of established plants or the construction of new plants.

But age and location are by no means the only determinants of competitive shift. The nature of an area's labor market, the cost and availability of land within its boundaries, its relation to the nation's ever-changing transportation network, the tax structure and financing possibilities it offers to new enterprises, and the degree to which it is able to offer services and facilities important to new manufacturing establishments—all these factors and many more help to determine a metropolitan area's advantage or disadvantage in holding its share of a particular industry or attracting a larger one.

New York and Pittsburgh: A Contrast

Differential rates of growth among metropolitan areas are explained in part by differences in industry mix and in part by competitive shifts in industry shares. But there is still another factor. It may be helpful to compare specifically the growth experiences of two major metropolitan areas: New York and Pittsburgh. Both are among the nation's oldest industrial centers, located in the northeastern quadrant of the country. Both owe their rise to industrial predominance to certain unique natural endowments: New York above all to its great Atlantic port, which long represented the major link between the sources of supply in the Old World and the markets of the United States; Pittsburgh to a combination of its rich endowments of fuel—chiefly coal and, to a lesser extent, natural gas—and its strategic location at the confluence of two major rivers (which won the city the title "Gateway to the West"). Both have seen the original advantage bestowed by their natural endowments eroded by technological change and by developments in the rest of the country. Both have watched their early specialties—New York, its flour-milling, copper- and sugar-refining, and all the manufacturing and commercial activities connected with its ports; Pittsburgh, its coal-mining and steel and glass production—either suffer a decline in national demand or disperse widely to other parts of the country. Yet the New York area has continued to expand at a healthy rate, while Pittsburgh's growth has all but ground to a halt. Why?

A careful study of the statistics reveals that New York's industry-mix is growing faster than the national average; Pittsburgh's, slower. But this is the beginning, not the end of the explanation. Despite the fact that its traditional industrial specialties have not kept pace with the over-all rate of national growth in recent decades and that its own share in them has been steadily shrinking as the process of dispersion continues, Pittsburgh's pattern of industrial specialization today does not differ radically from that of its economic heyday. Its heaviest specialization—now, as then—is in the production of iron, steel, metal, and glass, and in the manufacture of heavy industrial machinery and equipment. New York's production pattern, on the other hand, has changed radically. As its original specialties declined, others developed. By the end of the nineteenth century, New York was the nation's leader in the production of ready-to-wear apparel and in the printing and publishing industries. More recently, these specialties have been supplemented by still newer industrial concentrations: in aircraft, chemicals, electrical equipment, electronics, and scientific instruments. New York's industry mix is not fast-growing today because the area was lucky or far-sighted in its original industrial structure; rather, it possesses some particular attraction for new, rapidly expanding industries as such, which seems to insure that its industry mix, while constantly changing, will always be fast-growing, and that as its share of established specialties is gradually eroded, new ones will spring up to replace them.

The key, then, seems to be that New York has diversified its industrial structure, while Pittsburgh has been left clinging to its declining specialties. But what determines the degree of diversification—the ability to adjust to change and make the most of it? After all, an area does not choose its industries; in a free-enterprise economy, at least, the industries choose the area. The answer seems to lie in the type of atmosphere an area offers, and in the services and facilities it provides for industrial newcomers. New York has long since ceased to attract industries on the basis of specific natural endowments. Rather, it bases its appeal on the advantages of clustering—advantages in the form of a wide variety of specialized services in production, transportation, and marketing. These are the advantages which accrue, in certain types of industries, from being located close to one's competitors and to as many specialized business services as possible—services which a manufacturing firm would otherwise have to provide for itself. New York, with its heavy concentration of wholesale, retail, transportation, finance, communications, government, central office, and business and consumer service functions, offers a rich soil in which new industries can flourish.

Pittsburgh, on the other hand, offers a much thinner selection of such services, not only because it is smaller than New York, but because it has retained a degree of commitment to historic roots unusual in the mid-twentieth century. Having established its economy on the new, large-scale, heavy manufacturing industries in which it had a distinct natural advantage, Pittsburgh has continued to grow from this rather narrow base rather than branching out into the nonmanufacturing service sectors. While New York has a larger-than-average proportion of its total employment in the sectors described as "soil" for new industries, Pittsburgh's proportion in most of these sectors—with the exception of research and central office administration—is distinctly below average. It appears to be in the process of catching up with other metropolitan areas, but its long-standing handicap in this respect helps to explain why, as its original advantages have declined in importance and the industrial special-ties founded on them have declined or dispersed, new industries have not sprung up in their place fast enough to maintain a satis-factory over-all rate of growth.

Pittsburgh is the subject of a three-volume report issued early this year by the Pittsburgh Regional Planning Association. The fla-vor of the findings is conveyed in the selection, "Pittsburgh Takes Stock of Itself," by Edgar M. Hoover, the man who directed the research summarized in these volumes. More than any other major metropolitan study, this one of Pittsburgh puts the spotlight on the economic structure of the area as a determinant of economic growth.

The attraction of a well-rounded business environment is greater for some industries than for others. Industries which are character-istically small in scale, highly competitive, and with unstandardized products are those which most urgently require outside services and facilities of many types. Only a handful of manufacturing in-dustries require such services once they are solidly established, but most of them do in the beginning. Thus, large metropolitan areas have traditionally acted as incubators for new products and new processes. It is in the early stages of technical development in a given industry that uncertainty about the future is at its greatest. It is then that what the metropolitan area has to offer is most im-portant to the new firm. By permitting the businessman to rely on already existing supplies of space, labor, and transportation, and on established financial facilities and business services, the metropolis permits him to keep his own commitment to a minimum without sacrificing any of the essential nonproductive ingredients which may spell the difference between success and failure. It is this incubator function which the New York metropolitan area performs super-latively well.

Today, as manufacturing industries are increasingly freed from dependence on raw material resources, and as the accelerating rate of technological change increases the degree of uncertainty associated with many lines of production, it is likely that more and more industries will become increasingly dependent on their external environment. This implies that the creation of a climate favorable to diversification, through the provision of a competent labor force and of the wide variety of the skills and facilities categorized as the service sectors, will play a larger and larger role in determining a particular area's growth rate. Insofar as the creation of such a climate involves an increase in the number of jobs in the service industries, it will of course contribute directly to the growth of employment as well, particularly since many of these industries are themselves highly sensitive to the existence of their counterparts (research establishments, for example, clearly prefer to locate where a cluster of such establishments already exists). In two ways, then —directly by creating more jobs and more income in response to an ever-increasing demand, and indirectly by enhancing an area's attractiveness to fast-growing manufacturing industries—the expansion of the nonproductive sectors of the metropolitan economy may prove the key to sustained growth.

SHIFTS WITHIN THE METROPOLIS

We have talked about two types of change fundamental to the economics of metropolitan areas: the trend toward increasing metropolitanization in the United States as a whole, and the determinants of shifts among metropolitan areas in the form of widely diverse growth experiences. But equally striking shifts have been taking place within metropolitan areas—changes in internal structure and composition which, particularly in the case of the older and larger areas, pose at least as many problems as do the broader shifts and are closely related to them.

There is nothing homogeneous about a metropolitan area. Each of them divides into at least two distinct parts: the urban core or central city, and the surrounding suburban ring (which often shades off into rural countryside at the outer edges or in pockets far from main transportation lines). In the largest areas, it is possible to make further breakdowns—to distinguish an "inner" and "outer" ring, for example—and in nearly all it is possible to identify the distinctive core of the core: the central city's central business district. Obviously, as a metropolitan area grows it must grow outward, since there are severe limitations on how far up or down it can go. Thus, in the process of growth, the relative importance of the urban core shrinks and that of the surrounding ring expands. This is in part a trick of statistics, for the boundaries of a metropolitan area are not fixed; they grow as the area grows, so that new acreages and populations are continually being annexed. But there is more to the outward shift than simple annexation. There is no question that particular people and particular jobs tend to move out of the central city into the surrounding ring, and that this flow is almost always greater than the flow in the opposite direction. Nor is it simply that the relative importance of the city shrinks and that of the suburbs grows uniformly in every direction; rather, the particular function and specialization pattern of each of these parts changes drastically, and in the process the whole complexion of the metropolitan area is altered.

In the larger metropolitan areas, at least, the proportion of population living within the central city has been falling since the beginning of the century. During the same period, or at least as far back as can be measured reliably—generally, since 1929—the central cities' share of certain important employment categories (manufacturing, wholesaling, retailing) has been falling with equal regularity. It is not possible to make any simple statement about the two parallel trends since they interact on and influence each other in a variety of complex ways. But, if the movement of population is assumed as given, it is easy to see why certain types of jobs naturally follow. If people move to the suburbs, the grocery stores, hardware stores, laundries, and hairdressers—the retail and personal service industries—inevitably accompany them, as in fact they have.

Shifts in Manufacturing

Manufacturing employment, however, provides the most solid evidence of an outward redistribution, gradual but steady, in the great majority of the principal metropolitan areas. No matter the

standard of measurement—the proportion of metropolitan area manufacturing jobs accounted for by the central city, the rate of manufacturing employment growth in the city and in the suburbs, or the
share of total employment accounted for by manufacturing in the
city and in the surrounding areas—there is no question that, over
the past fifty years, manufacturing has grown more rapidly in the
surrounding rings of the great metropolitan areas than in the central core. These changes cannot be explained directly by movements
of population; indeed, manufacturing employment is much more
likely to effect intrametropolitan shifts in the distribution of population than to be affected by them. Rather, these changes relate to
the kinds of advantages a manufacturing firm is likely to derive
from a central location, the way these advantages have changed
over time, and the types of manufacturing operation for which they
are most important.

The data on manufacturing employment show, with remarkable
consistency, that manufacturing firms located in the urban center
of a metropolitan area are smaller in average size than those located
on the periphery. This is no mere coincidence; it is intimately tied
up with the function which a central location performs for a manufacturing establishment. This is, in brief, to provide all the facilities
and services which a firm does not want to provide for itself: rental
space for the firm which does not want to buy or build; a large labor
market to supply appropriate workers to the firm which cannot im-
port or train its own; transportation facilities to establishments
which find it cheaper to make fractional use of existing facilities
than to supply their own; specialists who enable the manufacturer
to subcontract out almost any portion of its operations which it cannot economically perform itself; proximity to a cluster of competitors, which minimizes the need for marketing facilities. By locating
close to such a complex of outside facilities, the small firm can
reduce its handicap vis-à-vis its larger competitors, and the firm
operating at a high level of uncertainty can keep its commitments to
a minimum. And these suppliers who must, in turn, have a large
enough market to make their operations pay are inevitably found in
greatest abundance at the urban core.

In certain types of manufacturing industries, chiefly those producing unstandardized and continuously changing products—the apparel industry is an obvious example—the level of uncertainty remains forever high and the importance of external suppliers always great. But in many industries this dependence is transitional, to be outgrown as the firm expands. For such industries, the outward movement of firms is an integral part of the growth process itself—for as a firm moves from dependence on external services to reliance on scale economies derived from its own operations, the advantages of a central urban location tend to be increasingly overshadowed by its disadvantages.

The chief difficulty an urban firm is likely to encounter as it grows is lack of space. In most established urban centers, it is very difficult and expensive for a firm to expand efficiently. And as a firm reaches the size where it becomes more economical to provide for its own transportation needs than to rely on outside facilities, the problem of traffic congestion and lack of parking and loading space at its urban location may become acute. Thus the greater availability of open sites is probably the most important single factor underlying the move to the suburbs.

As firms grow up and move away from their urban origins, new ones spring up to take their place. But in recent decades the replacement has not been rapid enough to sustain a rate of manufacturing growth at the center equal to that in the rings; in many large metropolitan areas, in fact, the number of manufacturing jobs in the urban core has declined not only relatively but also absolutely. Technological changes have had something to do with this: first, the increase in transport flexibility which accompanied the development of trucking; and, more recently, the trend toward integrated, continuous production processes—processes which demand single-story, extensive plant layouts for greatest efficiency and thus increase the disadvantages of cramped, multistory structures. But probably even more important are the inevitable results of the growth-and-decay process. As the central city grows older and more congested, the expense of modernizing obsolescent structures increases until it becomes cheaper to build anew on open land than to modify exist-

ing structures. And as the shift to the periphery continues, the suburban areas develop industrial complexes of their own and are increasingly able to provide many of the services which were once
the exclusive characteristic of the urban center. More and more
fledgling firms may be attracted to a suburban location, rather than
waiting to move there after they reach a particular stage of expansion.

Many of the forces which tend to push manufacturing operations
out of the metropolitan center and into the rings also affect wholesaling operations, although the outward shift in this sector has so
far been less pronounced. Obsolescent inner-city structures, changed
transportation networks, and the horizontal-layout demands of modern goods-handling methods are causing a more rapid growth of
wholesaling employment at the periphery than in the urban center.

Population, manufacturing, retailing, household services, and—to
a lesser extent—wholesaling are all moving out of the central city.
Yet the central cities show no signs of emptying—many, in fact,
seem more congested and densely packed than ever. What is filling
the vacuum? In part, the answer lies in the discussion of manufacturing. The centers of most of the large metropolitan areas continue to attract "exotic," highly competitive types of manufacturing.
But there is another type of function, increasingly important in
twentieth-century society, in which both inputs and outputs are
even more heterogeneous and unstandardized, rapid communication
and face-to-face contacts even more important than for the exotic
manufacturing industries. These are the highly specialized areas of
finance, business services, and central office administration, whose
inputs are skill or knowledge or information, whose outputs are not
goods but service or advice or decisions. It is these establishments
—banks and law offices, advertising agencies and central administrative offices, consulting firms and government agencies—which
are filling more and more of the central cities of most urban areas,
and are becoming the primary function of the core of the core, the
city's central business district.

This, then, is the general pattern of employment in the modern
metropolis: a central urban core which dominates the surrounding

rings in the performance of office, financial, and business service functions and which also houses those types of manufacturing, wholesaling, and retailing in which the need for maximum opportunities for face-to-face contacts with suppliers or customers or both provides a strong incentive for clustering. Surrounding it is the suburban ring or rings, attracting an increasing share of the manufacturing and wholesaling activities in the area, as well as those retailing and household service operations designed to satisfy routine, day-to-day demands. At the outer fringes of the metropolitan area there is likely to be a certain amount of activity dependent on the soil—activities which are likely to be dying off rapidly unless they are of the sort essential to the well-being of the metropolitan dwellers themselves, such as dairy farms or truck gardens.

Population Shifts

Certain types of jobs have been moving out of the metropolitan areas for many decades; the people, in most cases, began moving out even earlier. The history of any city reveals a continuous outward flight of residents, as inventions and changing tastes make once-satisfactory dwellings obsolescent and as industrial and commercial operations encroach on them, making renovation difficult and expensive and threatening them with crowding and dirt and noise. Generally, it is the well-off who move first and farthest in search of space and fresh air and privacy. By the early years of this century, the development of streetcar and subway lines made it increasingly possible for the middle classes to follow and, in the years since World War II, the ubiquity of automobile ownership has greatly accelerated an exodus emphasized by postwar suburban housing developments ringing nearly every metropolitan area. As one group moves outward, its place in the abandoned and obsolescent residential areas is generally taken by a group one step lower on the economic ladder, so that socioeconomic levels tend to drop steadily toward an area's core. In some of the older metropolitan areas, in fact, the process has gone one step further; not only have the rich and the people of moderate means moved out, abandoning urban residence to those too poor to move, but the slums themselves have begun to creep outward, creating an absolute decline in the city's population.

These generalizations, however, conceal the wide variety of patterns actually found among the metropolitan areas of the United States. Depending on the particular stage of development and pattern of specialization, metropolitan areas differ tremendously in the distribution of their activities and their inhabitants. For some, the outward shift of population and jobs has spelled the absolute decline of the central city; for others, it has signaled the opportunity for a huge boom of renovation and office-building construction at the core, as the city adjusts itself to its new and specialized functions. In some areas, important manufacturing industries have good reason to cling to their location at the core (Manhattan's garment industry is an example); in others, the industrial mix is such that virtually all manufacturing operations are heeding the outward pull. Some central cities still harbor large residential areas in which new middle- and upper-class housing is being built; in others, almost the only residents are the slum-dwellers and the only residences are the crumbling structures they have taken over from the more fortunate, perhaps interspersed with a few apartment-enclaves of those well-to-do whose very special kinds of housing needs can be satisfied by high-rise buildings.

Conflicting Trends

When all the infinite variety has been taken into account, metropolitan areas still face a set of common problems—problems which act as barriers to their orderly growth. One is the severe imbalance frequently created by the outward shifts in population and employment. As many types of jobs move into the periphery, the central cities are becoming more and more specialized in functions which require chiefly professional, technical, and clerical workers—a skilled and literate work force. But the skilled and literate groups are precisely those segments of the population which are increasingly choosing to live outside the urban center. The slum-dwellers.

on the other hand, are poorly suited to fill the city's office and service jobs; the jobs for which they are suited—the less skilled occupations involved in many types of manufacturing, wholesaling, and household service operations—are moving farther and farther away from them.

The increased cross-hauling of people this imbalance implies represents at best an increased expenditure of time and resources, often complicated by the growing traffic congestion in many metropolitan areas. But it may mean more than that. By reducing the availability of an appropriate labor force, it can make both suburbs and city less attractive to new establishments in the relevant sectors. And it can leave the city slum-dwellers stranded, raising the unemployment rate and the welfare burden which must be borne by the area's center.

In many metropolitan areas, the increasing traffic congestion makes it harder and harder to carry out many functions efficiently within the urban core, and harder and harder to get into the center from the periphery. A related difficulty is the increasing expense of reclaiming obsolescent structures and outmoded sites, an expense which not only works against the return of the middle-class or affluent city-dweller, but also reduces the attractiveness of urban locations for nonresidential uses. These are, of course, primarily problems of the central city. But the problems of the city are inevitably the problems of the metropolitan area as well, for despite the increasing importance of the suburban sections, the economic well-being of any metropolitan area is still heavily dependent on the city around which it has grown. The movement toward complementary specialization of functions in city and suburb serves, in fact, to increase the interdependence between the two.

METROPOLITAN PROBLEMS

These are some of the major pressures operating to check the growth of metropolitan areas—a growth which is being fed by strong pressures of its own. In some areas these difficulties have already become acute; in others they will not have to be faced for

many years to come. But they are problems with which every metropolitan area, sooner or later, will have to deal; the more fortunate
or far-sighted ones preventively, others in search of a cure or at least
a palliative.

Modern man does not attribute all his dissatisfaction with the
world around him to his metropolitan abode. But the metropolis
does get tagged for more than its fair share of his gripes. No doubt,
the new spatial arrangements have created new problems and intensified others which existed before. But the metropolis is also
indicted for problems which are revealed rather than fostered by
the new spatial patterns.

Crime, delinquency, perversion, poverty, slums: all these have become more visible and therefore seemingly more acute. It is easier
to count noses in the city than in the country. The density dimension
—squalor per square mile—adds urgency to a problem which is
fundamentally measured by the frequency of its occurrence among
people.

The distinction between the emergence of a new problem and
the revelation of an old one will help to focus attention on those
problems which are uniquely metropolitan in character. The resolution of old problems in the new setting is a challenge worthy of
attention.

Some further distinctions are in order. Dissatisfaction with the
current state of affairs implies one or more of three essentially different kinds of judgments. The most basic is a value judgment
which challenges the wisdom of the current allocation of resources
among competing needs. "We will master space travel before we
solve the commuting problem, and isn't that idiotic?" is an indictment of the values which seem to prevail in Congress. The argument is that the solution of the metropolitan transportation problem
would yield social benefits greater than those conferred upon society
by the space program. Galbraith is making a similar value judgment
when he argues that an affluent society should devote more of its
wealth to the alleviation of pressing social problems.

The popular discontent with the quality of life in the metropolitan areas is basically of this character. More should be spent to
improve housing, to relieve traffic congestion, to control air pol-

lution, to provide adequate recreational facilities. More should be allocated to these needs even if it means less can be allocated to other national programs.

One hesitates to debate values because they do not necessarily rest on tidy logical arguments. But one is entitled to ask whether the devotion of more resources to these problems would indeed bring us that much closer to their solution. Could we profitably spend another $5 billion on the alleviation of urban problems? We know how to get to the moon, or—to put it more accurately—we know how to learn how to get to the moon and how to get there if the funds are made available. Can we say the same for progress toward the solution of problems of the metropolitan area? No one will deny that we have made progress in our understanding of the mechanics of metropolitan development and in the design of instruments to guide that development along desirable lines. But how fast can we accelerate this process of discovery and engineering with additional funds?

This brings up the second class of gripes which are implicit in many criticisms of metropolitan form. Are we using our resources efficiently? If we add up the total social effort in the metropolis— federal, state, local, private—couldn't we get better results for the same expenditure if we were more efficient in the management of our resources? A classic argument along these lines: If we spent less on roads and more on rapid transit we could get more transportation capacity for a given expenditure on transportation. Another: If we spent less money on tearing down old buildings and more on their rehabilitation we could get more urban renewal for a given expenditure.

This is a more subtle attack on the way we manage our affairs and is more characteristic of the academic than of the common man. But many private interests have a stake in the argument and they contribute to its vigor.

Finally, there are those who challenge the very goals which are implicit in current programs to improve the metropolitan milieu. The planners who decry suburban "sprawl" will fortify their arguments with complaints of inefficiency but fundamentally they are against this way of life because they feel it does not contribute to

the improvement of society and the progress of civilization. Recent
tirades against current fashions in urban renewal are also in this
vein.

THE METROPOLITAN TRANSPORTATION PROBLEM

These general observations bear upon almost any issue which is
hotly debated on the metropolitan scene. But transportation and the
pattern of land use are at the heart of the metropolitan problem.
One cannot be adequately treated without the other, since the interdependence of the two is intense.

What are the elements of the metropolitan transportation problem? Economists are fond of sorting things into two hoppers which
they call *supply* and *demand*. Sometimes this framework is strained
and artificial, but let's see how far it will fit this problem.

The Demand for Transportation

The demand for transportation is generated by what we might
call, for lack of a better term, *spatial specialization*. Certain areas
are best suited to industry; some, to people; others, most suitable
for shopping; still others, for recreation, and so on. The superiority
in each case may rest on natural features, or on the simple fact that
it is efficient to concentrate an activity in one place—say, downtown. But, no matter the reason, the fact is that a complete scale
of activities for the average citizen—work, leisure, shopping, recreation—can be put together only by bridging the distance which
separates the locations where these functions are performed. This
simple fact gives rise to a demand for transportation. Of special
significance for this discussion is the added fact that the complete
package most often—though not always—embraces frequent movements among places not encompassed within one political jurisdiction in the metropolitan area. Thus transportation is a metropolitan
problem.

1. *The dominance of the journey to work.*
From the point of view of engineering efficiency alone, the demands
imposed upon the metropolitan transportation system by the journey to

work seem disproportionate. In this context, the entire system must be designed to fill a demand which exists for only two or three hours per day.

But no other single journey is equal in importance to the journey to work, for "work"—whatever form it may take—is the means whereby the society functions and perpetuates itself. Therefore, it is clear that nothing must prevent a significant segment of the population from reaching its place of work. In this light, the need for meeting the demands imposed upon a transportation system by rush-hour traffic begins to take on its proper aspect.

Consideration has been given to solving the problem by staggering the hours of work among different groups of the employed population. However, such a view does not take into account two factors. First, work hours are already staggered to a considerable degree. Day-laborers generally start their day between 7:00 and 8:00 A.M.; manufacturing plants start their day between 8:00 and 9:00 A.M.; and most white-collar workers start between 9:00 and 9:30 A.M. (The close of the eight-hour day is staggered accordingly.) Second, this view does not take into account the daily family routine of the commuting suburbanite and city-worker, one in which an early homecoming plays an important part and one which cannot be simply altered by efficiency considerations. It must be assumed, therefore, that as long as residence and place of employment remain separated by a journey's distance, the rush-hour is here to stay.

2. *Other mass movements in the metropolitan area*

  a. *Movement to shopping centers*

   A substantial part of the retail establishments selling garments, household goods, and other nongrocery items is located in nonresidential areas, and thus requires shoppers to travel to them. In addition, the large percentage of two-car suburban families has enabled suburban supermarkets to locate some distance from residential sections, often in general shopping centers. The journey to shop thus constitutes a significant movement in the metropolitan area today, both into and out of the center city and, more diffusely, throughout the suburbs.

  b. *Movement to cultural and recreational centers*

   This movement has many forms, comprising

   (1) Individual daytime movements which are mostly random in character, becoming massive only on special occasions: ballgames, special shows, large conventions, and so on, when these occur during the week.

(2) Evening movements, primarily to entertainment districts, which are still substantially located in the center city in most metropolitan areas.

(3) Weekend movements, varied in nature, including travel to special events such as public games, parades, parks, and zoos, as well as social visits.

(4) Seasonal movements, which create changing patterns, such as the influx of vacationers into the center city, travel to local beaches and parks, and so on.

c. *Random movement*

On top of these fairly regular and sizable movements there are the numerous trips by individuals going about their individual concerns. The job-seeker going to an interview; the patient going to the doctor; the guest coming from a visit—all constitute a significant and constant part of the transport-using public. By the nature of individual movements, these can be seen as randomly distributed over the area, varying from hour to hour and from day to day.

d. *The movement of goods*

Although the movement of goods does not conventionally constitute an aspect of the metropolitan transportation problem, the fact that the same highways and streets, and to some extent, other modes of metropolitan transport, are used for this purpose makes it a relevant factor. Since this "movement" thus affects the total demand for transportation services, it must be taken into account in any realistic appraisal of the transportation problem.

These significant ingredients of demand do not add up to a fixed or unique or stable set of transport requirements. Just as hunger underlies the demand for food but does not determine its exact magnitude, so the need to travel and move about does not uniquely determine the demand for transport. People can eat more or less and they can travel more or less. How much transportation they elect to "consume" will depend also on how much it costs in relation to their capacity to bear these costs and the value which they place on this and other items in their budget.

This point may appear to be distressingly obvious, yet it has been overlooked by a large number of transportation planners who behave as if the transportation needs of the metropolis are uniquely determined by spatial arrangements and their only concern is to devise a system which will meet these requirements at minimum cost. Thus they overlook the fact that individuals can—within limits —control their transport requirements by controlling their choice of locations, their choice of activities, and the frequency with which they indulge in them, and that all these decisions are affected by the transportation costs which they confront in selecting among alternative patterns. Give them a free four-lane highway and they will make decisions based on the cost of gasoline and car mainte- nance. Give them a rapid transit system with a thirty-cent fare and they will make decisions based on radically different calculations.

In rebuttal, these planners argue that experience shows that man's travel habits are quite stable and predictable. Give them enough information about a family—income, and the age and oc- cupation of its members—and they will deduce a transport package: so many work trips, so many shopping trips, so many miscellaneous trips per day or week. Give them this information on all the families in the metropolitan area, and tell them where the jobs, the resi- dences, the shopping centers, and all other activities are located, and they will put it all in a computer, press the button, and in a matter of minutes, reveal the whole pattern of movement. Then the engineers begin to work to design the "necessary" capacity.

The counterargument is simple. It is always a fallacy to argue from what is to what inevitably must be. Where people live and work not only determines transport needs, but is also determined by the transportation system—how much and at what price. The formulae developed to convert persons and cars into trips reflect the quantity demanded given the existing transport system. They do not reveal the kind of responses which another set of alternatives would evoke.

Why Subsidize Transport?

There is still another implicit judgment in transport thinking which needs to be made explicit. This relates to the question of subsidy and the use of inappropriate charges for the use of the serv- ice. It is a rare situation indeed in which the users of a transport facility pay for its entire cost. Rapid transit systems are almost universally subsidized. The rule of thumb is that users should pay for operating costs while the entire community should bear the capital costs through general taxation. Highways are paid for out of gasoline taxes and give the appearance of not being subsidized by the general public. But this is an illusion which is quickly shattered when subjected to the most rudimentary analysis. The over-all balance between highway costs and gasoline tax revenues—assuming it works out that way—is irrelevant to the main issue: Does the user confront a price which reflects the cost to society of accommodating his desire to travel at a particular time on a particular road?

Once a man has filled his tank and paid his tax he confronts the same price whether he travels during the rush hour—when his presence contributes to the strain on the system—or in the middle of the night when the only cost to society is the infinitesimal wear and tear of the surface occasioned by his trip. True, he is deterred during the rush hour by congestion and in this sense he pays a higher price for the use of the highway at that time, but he is not deterred by the fact that his fellow-travelers are also annoyed by the congestion which is aggravated by his being on the highway at that time. Put it this way: The whole class of peak-hour travelers whose demand determined the size of the highway faces the same price as the off-peak travelers whose demand could readily be satisfied by a less expensive highway. It is just as if everyone paid the same premium for fire insurance despite the great discrepancies in potential loss among different customers or, to get closer to home, as if everyone paid the same price for cars even if some prefer limousines and others prefer compacts.

As a rule we believe in giving the individual the incentive to buy cheaper products by offering them to him at lower prices; we expect people to pay for their expensive tastes. We like to think that the difference in price reflects the difference in cost to society of providing the two sets of products. Not so in transportation. Why?

One answer often given is simply that it would be terribly expensive administratively to enforce a "proper" set of prices. The problems do appear to be very complex. The fact is, however, that rough approximations to ideal prices are not difficult to achieve in particular cases, although the attempt is not made. For example, it seems reasonable that tolls—where they exist—could be varied at a modest cost to reflect the intensity of use at different times. Parking meters are used to impose a price during certain hours and not others, but the potentialities for the application of this principle are far greater than that. As Lyle Fitch suggests in the selection, "Metropolitan Financial Problems," the scope for the application of user charges in lieu of general taxation is far greater than most people tend to assume.

No, feasibility is not the ultimate issue. Rather, it is that down deep we believe that mobility is like education—we want people to have more of it than they are willing to pay for directly and we do not want the rich to be able to outbid the poor. If the poor man can stand the congestion he can slug it out with the rich man and the rich man can't bribe the poor man to stay off the road. And we want both of them to travel more than they would choose to if they had to pay the full cost of providing the service.

What are the subtle gains from increased mobility which the individual either cannot perceive or cannot capture for himself? Improved access within the metropolitan area accomplishes two objectives: it permits greater concentration of particular functions in particular places by extending the market which can be served from a given point, and it confers greater freedom on individuals in locating themselves with reference to these points. When the New York subways were built, the labor-supply area for the garment district and the market area for the large department stores were dramatically extended. By the same token, the worker was now able to reside in the Bronx and Brooklyn and offer his labor and his earnings in the Manhattan area. For a small increment in travel costs, he gained the freedom to settle in a more attractive residential setting.

The rationale for not asking the subway rider to bear the entire social cost of the service was fairly clear. Faced with a higher price, more people would choose to avoid the trip by settling close to their work. The private cost of this decision—high rents and slum conditions—would be more than offset by the cost of transportation.

But the social cost of that decision would be higher because many of the consequences of congested living weigh more heavily on society than on the individual. Thus, society, as it were, put a greater value on the opportunity to disperse the population than did individuals. Society's demand for transport was therefore additive to the individual's demand and the combined demand justified a system more costly than users would pay for.

So one reason for subsidizing mobility is that it leads to a more desirable pattern of settlement. But there are other excuses for subsidy. Improved access increases the scope for specialization, and specialization makes for greater efficiency. The individual who participates either as a vendor or a customer benefits from this efficiency in higher incomes or lower prices. He should be willing to pay for the cost of improving access which leads to these benefits. The Wall Street broker and the investor both profit from the intense concentration of the securities business in a small area. But as individuals they cannot perceive the effect on the efficiency of the total industry of their private decision to relate to this market. So they have to be induced—as the farmer was induced to go West by cheap railroad transportation.

There is still a third element in the argument for subsidy. When people get together, they generate benefits to society which they cannot wholly capture for themselves. If a man is stimulated by his friends to develop an idea which he can turn to a profit, they don't necessarily have any claims upon him. They will share the benefits in no greater measure than will society at large. Society, therefore, has a stake in this contact over and above that of the direct participants and is therefore willing to pay part of the cost of enhancing mobility and increasing the probability that such fruitful contacts will occur.

It would seem that there is a rather impressive case for subsidizing mobility. Yet there is room for considerable skepticism and serious debate. All the benefits one can conjure up, added together, will not make the case for subsidy, unless these benefits are continually being amplified and extended by further improvements in access. If a two-lane highway fully exhausts these benefits, then a four-lane highway can be justified only in terms of the demands of peak-hour travelers. If they are charged a price which does not cover the incremental cost of a four-lane highway, the extra social costs will exceed the extra social benefits and an improper expenditure of public funds will have been made.

We can't make final judgments; we can only pose relevant questions. Are we really convinced that the transportation investments we are now making are encouraging the kind of land-use patterns we desperately want to achieve in the metropolitan area? Can we be sure that the further gains from increased specialization—even if they exist—are worth the extra costs? Finally, do we need to facilitate contact between individuals further, or have we exhausted this fountain of social gain?

It may very well be that subsidizing transport is a habit we have developed which has lost its *raison d'être*. We may want to revive an older habit—which is to let private gain dictate the allocation of resources.

On the Supply Side of Transportation

So much for demand. Much of the uneasiness about metropolitan transportation stems from the supply side, where some serious biases seem to be distorting the true technological alternatives. A hot debate rages as to the relative merits of different modes of transport —rail, bus, automobile, monorail, and others. Various estimates of the cost and performance of each mode have been generated by special interests and (alas!) by objective scholars as well.

Unfortunately, we cannot dispel the smoke and reveal the truth. All we can do here, as before, is to focus on some principles and raise some questions. Just as the individual rider or driver does not always confront prices which reflect costs, so communities making choices among alternative transport investments do not confront prices which properly reflect costs. The simple fact is that highway construction is heavily financed by the federal government, which bears 90 per cent of the cost of mileage on the interstate system and 50 per cent of the cost of other primary roads. The municipality is further shielded by the state, which matches federal grants and provides additional financing for other roads without federal participation.

No such munificence is extended to mass transit systems or commuter railroads. Recently there have been some gestures in this direction by the federal government and some state governments, but the magnitudes are minuscule by comparison. So a much larger share of nonhighway investments must be borne by the community. This naturally sets up a bias in favor of highways.

But is the bias necessarily unjustified? If the financial participation of higher levels of government in roads reflects a social valuation greater than the community's then roads are really cheaper to a community because they are available as a by-product of state and federal investments. By the same token, if the community alone has a stake in rail systems then it should regard these as truly more expensive from a social point of view.

It is doubtful, however, that the difference between the national and the community stake in highways is anywhere near the proportions suggested by the financial arrangements. The overwhelming proportion of traffic on federal roads in any metropolitan area is local in origin and destination. The through traffic certainly does not call for more capacity than is required to satisfy local traffic.

It seems difficult to avoid the conclusion, therefore, that the cards are stacked in favor of highways for noneconomic reasons. Given the magnitude of the bias, it must surely be true that other transport modes would have been preferred in many instances if the real economic costs were properly reflected in the alternatives faced by the community.

Federal and state subsidies aside, the bias toward highways is caused by a pervasive underaccounting of the total costs of such services. A comprehensive budget for a new highway from the outskirts to the downtown area, for example, would include not only the costs of building the highway but also the costs of accommodating the additional traffic in the city, repairing the wear and tear on the streets, and providing the extra police, the extra traffic signals, and the extra storage or parking space. A projected highway investment is rarely viewed in this comprehensive way because responsibility for each of these parts of the total transport package is generally vested in different decision-making bodies. The Highway Department makes the highway decision, the Parking Authority makes the parking decision, while the city government passively reacts to pressure on its police force.

By contrast, when a projected rapid transit system is estimated, all these aspects are more fully taken into account. The cost of stations and terminals in the densely developed downtown area weighs heavily in the calculations. The total costs are therefore more realistic and higher standards of revenue and social benefit are imposed to justify the expense.

On the reasoning developed here, many economists and planners have concluded that greater investment in rapid transit facilities and reduced expenditures on highways would be more consistent with the underlying economics of the transportation problem. But some have vigorously resisted this point of view. One such person is Professor John R. Meyer, whose analysis is found in the selection "Knocking Down the Straw Men."

These difficulties are compounded by a central fact of metropolitan life: numerous independent political jurisdictions are independently making decisions on the very manifestation of their interdependence—the transport arteries which make them accessible one to the other and greatly influence the character of the interrelationships between them.

LAND-USE PLANNING

Economic forces and transportation policy are major factors in determining the shape of metropolitan areas. But there are those who refuse to let it go at that. These are the city and regional planners whose principal article of faith is that spatial destinies can be shaped by wise and courageous planning. The axiom which inspires them is that laissez-faire cannot, except by accident, lead to a socially acceptable allocation of space in the metropolitan area.

No one can seriously question this axiom. Of all the decisions made in pursuit of private gain, those which relate to the use of land are most likely to confer costs and/or benefits on one's neighbors which are normally not taken into account in the individual's calculations. By my decision, I may affect my neighbor directly by increasing or diminishing the value of his property. I may affect him directly by increasing or diminishing the costs to the community of providing public services.

What is true of individuals in the city is true of communities in the metropolitan area. If a factory in one community pollutes the atmosphere over a larger area, the community cannot be allowed to decide for itself whether the control of such pollution is socially desirable.

A whole arsenal of weapons has been put at the disposal of our planners to help them in their struggle. One of them—and the most direct one—is *zoning*. In most cities and metropolitan areas, local government is empowered to deny the private citizen the right to develop his own land as he wishes. Proposed uses must conform to the community's criteria for appropriate development and be consistent with its over-all or comprehensive plan.

A second weapon is *code enforcement*. After a structure has been approved for a particular site, the community may still intervene to guarantee that minimum standards of construction and main‑ tenance are met to protect the safety and property of all citizens.

A third instrument is *taxation*. This is an indirect control. By using its discretion in setting tax rates and making assessments, the community can influence the pattern of land use through the market mechanism. It can penalize undesirable uses and subsidize that kind of use which the city wants to encourage.

The most powerful weapon is the *right to condemn private property* and pre-empt it for public purposes. These purposes are not limited to the construction of public facilities such as government buildings, streets, or parks; they include the redevelopment of property through private auspices, as in the case of urban renewal.

Finally, the community is empowered to *make direct investments* which contribute to the total pattern of land use by the construction of public housing and industrial and commercial properties later leased to private citizens.

With this package of prerogatives, planners might be expected to exude a greater sense of confidence in their power and greater pride in their achievements. There might also be expected among citizens a stronger feeling that their destiny is in competent hands. It is impossible to measure the success of planning in objective terms. What is observable is considerable malaise on both sides. The planners and their charges both exhibit frustration. Perhaps the frustration is wholly unjustified in the light of solid achievements. But it suggests there may be some serious misgivings about the whole venture. These are perhaps nowhere better articulated than in the selection by Dr. Vernon in "The Myth and Reality of Our Urban Problems."

The Influence of Social Science

One common source of frustration is the failure of the planner to pay due respect to the forces outside his control. After all is said and done, the determination of land-use patterns remains largely in private hands. Households and businesses and private institutions continue to make most of fundamental investment decisions: to build here and tear down there; to vacate this lot and occupy that one. Through regulation and public investment, the planner can, at best, only influence the total pattern. He cannot dictate it so long as there remains any semblance of free enterprise in the market for land.

The corollary is that planners must understand how private decisions will be affected by public intervention. This argues for the injection of social scientific understanding in the planning process and greater emphasis on social science research to supplement progress in the development of the planning arts.

The idea has been accepted by the planning profession, but not without some distortions. (Very often the convert's zeal frightens the missionary.) After having shunned the social scientist in the beginning, some planners have turned to worshiping his omnipotence and have been disappointed when their prayers went unanswered. Once a relevant relationship is pointed out to him, the planner wants its exact specifications—tomorrow. He can't bear to remain uncertain about the implications of his new-found wisdom.

The relation between social science and planning has also been confused by a naïve hunger for prophecy and an ample supply of false prophets. The 1950's witnessed a rash of studies designed to reveal the future: how many people, how many jobs, what kinds of jobs, where will people be living, where will they be working— in 1985! The planner was entranced by the prospect of having his domain projected into the distant future so he could properly and realistically plan for it. Much of this activity was surely beneficial, but the diversion was costly and unjustified for a number of reasons —least of which was the unreliability of the estimates. The fact is the planner could do no better for the city in the crystal ball than he could for the real city before his eyes. He was daydreaming when he should have been hard at work.

The whole concept of planning for 1985, or any specific future date, is now in disrepute. True, some very costly mistakes can be made if the future is not reckoned with. But such mistakes are not avoided by behaving as if the future were known with certainty and in great detail. Instead, the planner is now groping for a strategy which permits the future to unfold without invalidating too much of the past. This entails a commitment to planning as an ongoing process. The plan must never be "finished"; it must continually be modified and amplified as new data, new knowledge, and new experiences are exposed. And the greatest challenge the planner faces now is that of constructing a mechanism to capture the new information and quickly extract its implications for planning policy.

The Planner Is Not in the Saddle

A second source of anxiety about the planning process is the absence of effective coordination between planners and other city officials whose decisions have important consequences for land use. The fact is that all the powers listed above are not typically vested in the planning agency. Except for zoning, the regulatory powers usually reside elsewhere—and so does the taxing power.

Initiative for public construction and the condemnation of private property for redevelopment very often also rests with other agencies. To insure a consistent public strategy in land use, the planning agency would need to command considerable respect and power within the city administration. Unfortunately, this is not often the case. Most city officials regard the planner as an academician who should be expected to support political decisions but not really to shape them in any significant way.

A third problem arises out of the bias—as in the case of transportation policy—introduced by the availability of federal and state funds which can be used for certain purposes only. Many people consider urban renewal and city planning synonymous because they see urban renewal as the major "concrete" manifestation of planning. And to the extent that this is true, it reflects the simple fact that urban renewal is heavily financed by Uncle Sam.

Condemnation, clearance, and redevelopment—all of which are elements in the planner's total strategy for effectuating a more desirable land-use pattern—are most readily financed when they can be combined in an urban renewal package. In round figures, the federal government will bear two thirds of the net cost of the project. The local government is naturally under pressure to make the most of these opportunities, and only a very courageous planner can protect the integrity of his plan against these encroachments. If his plans call for a greater reliance on local funds and a lesser reliance on federal and state funds, his chances are slim. Yet when the federal funds have been spent and the new project is completed, the planning agency is necessarily identified with it, for better or for worse.

The federal government will not finance an urban renewal project unless the city can demonstrate that it has a plan of which this project is an integral part. But this provision is hardly adequate to insure that a city is using urban renewal to further its goals and not shaping its goals to maximize urban renewal. This is no reflection on the perspicacity of federal officials. They simply cannot be expected to serve as superplanners who know what's best for every city in the country. They can only ask for evidence of planning consciousness in the community.

Recognition of this fundamental conflict between local planning goals and the goals of the federal urban renewal effort is manifested in the emergence of a new concept of federal support. Rather than have the federal government approve specific projects, the new policy would call for a federal appropriation of x dollars to be put entirely at the disposal of local authorities once the federal government was satisfied with the integrity of the over-all plan. In this way, the principle of federal support could be maintained but its distorting effect minimized.

Perhaps the greatest trouble with planning is the confusion of goals. What values is the planner trying to maximize? There is a long list of desirable objectives from which to choose: better housing opportunities for all citizens, a more attractive physical environment, the improvement of the city's tax base, the enlargement of employment opportunities in the local economy, a "strong" downtown, more open space for parks, minimum strain on the city's operating budget—and many others. These objectives are not necessarily inconsistent, but they can't all be pursued at the same time with equal vigor; one must be prepared to make judgments as to priorities. Yet the impulse is strong to maintain a posture of moving forward on all fronts.

Not the least of the planner's problems is that there are too many of them. There are big-city planners and small-town planners, regional planners and county planners. There is enough work for all of them, but their efforts are not additive in terms of a total strategy for the metropolitan area as a whole. This brings up once more the question of overlapping jurisdictions.

INTERGOVERNMENTAL RELATIONS

The generic problem of the metropolitan area is the political one of reconciling the conflicting goals and interests of independent communities which affect each other's welfare. Difficulties inherent in working out solutions to the problems of a metropolitan area are complicated by the nature of local political systems, both formal and informal. The task of coordinating policy among special district, town, city, county, state, and federal governmental units is complicated further by the interplay of political parties or other power centers on the various levels. The most efficient or technically desirable method of handling a particular metropolitan problem may have to be set aside in favor of a method which is politically feasible.

A variety of administrative alternatives has been proposed to facilitate action on a metropolitan basis. These proposals range from the retention of ultimate control by each political unit to the destruction of the integrity of previously existing units and the substitution of a new, metropolitan government.

1. *Annexation,* as its name implies, is the legal process through which a city adds territory to which it must provide services anyway. Annexation has generally been accomplished by ordinance rather than by referendum. A recent example is Knoxville, which annexed forty-one square miles of territory and, in so doing, increased its population from 47,756 to 179,973. Annexation may transform metropolitan problems into municipal ones and may eliminate the necessity for coordination among governmental units at a particular moment. But there are two serious limitations to this approach: (1) a city can annex territory only until its boundaries reach those of a municipality which refuses to be annexed; and (2) a municipality will again be faced with a problem of metropolitan administration when it reaches state boundaries, if its services extend into the neighboring state or states.

A related alternative is the granting of extraterritorial powers by state legislatures to cities to enable them to extend their jurisdiction beyond municipal limits for certain purposes.

2. *City-county consolidation* has been attempted to increase the scope of the administrative machinery required to handle problems of a metropolitan nature. Although this consolidation of administrative machinery may prove to be of value to some areas, it can never provide the whole answer to this problem, because almost half the standard metropolitan areas contain more than one county.

This approach has not been widespread. In fact, the recent Nashville and Davidson County (Tennessee) merger is one of the few successful attempts at such consolidation in well over a decade. Other efforts in recent years have failed.

3. *County amalgamation,* which, for example, is permitted in the new Michigan state constitution, provides the opportunity for two or more counties in a metropolitan area to combine personnel, money, and other resources for greater efficiency. Where county boundaries correspond to the boundaries of the metropolitan area

as they do in the Tri-County area of Michigan (which includes the state capital), this approach facilitates efficient planning for and administration of the services of the area.

4. *Municipal federation,* as in the case of the famous Toronto Metropolitan Government, has been attempted successfully and provides an organization through which representatives of the municipalities concerned may handle matters important to the efficient management of the metropolis as a whole.

The use of federation either on the county or the municipal level is limited, of course, in that the metropolis may eventually extend beyond the limits of the counties or municipalities concerned. When extension of services beyond the boundaries of the existing federation becomes necessary, the problem again arises of whether to annex, contract to cooperate, or create a new body to handle the pertinent problems.

A variety of other approaches has been attempted or suggested which circumvent the need to handle metropolitan problems through the machinery of existing local governments.

A. *Regional authorities* have been created to deal with particular problems. Although authorities such as the Port of New York Authority may escape the geographical, administrative, and financial limitations characteristic of local governments, they are themselves limited by the fact that they are authorized to deal only with a particular problem. Related problems which may be of vital concern to the specialized regional authority remain in the province of the region's existing local governments.

B. *Voluntary councils* have been created to provide forums for the discussion of metropolitan problems. In fact, the American Municipal Association and the National Association of Counties have formed a joint service to encourage the formation of such councils on a city-county basis.

C. *Federal government action* has, in some instances, either encouraged or precluded the necessity of action on a metropolitan basis. Problems related to essential services which are common from one metropolitan area to another may logically be considered as the concern of the national government. Within appropriate agencies or committees of the federal government, it is possible to bring both intellectual and financial resources to bear on problems which individual metropolitan areas could not afford to tackle with a satisfactory degree of efficiency. These agencies or committees, if only by virtue of their centralized location, can provide the most accessible and most efficient source for assistance to scattered areas with common problems. It is important to note, however, that the existence of an agency or committee within the national government to deal with an individual metropolitan problem does not preclude the necessity for machinery on the local level through which the federal assistance may be applied.

The recent attempt to establish a separate Department of Urban Affairs and Housing in the federal government is indicative of the growing recognition that efforts to cope with metropolitan problems need to be more closely coordinated than they have been in the past.

THE ECONOMICS OF POLITICAL ALTERNATIVES

Does the economist have anything to contribute to the evaluation of these alternative political arrangements? The temptation is to recommend the obliteration of municipal boundaries in favor of more "efficient" metropolitan government. But, if the economist has one lesson to teach, it is that efficiency is not a technological or engineering concept. Efficiency has to do with the conversion of resources to the satisfaction of human demands. We can't measure how *much* we are getting for our efforts except as we attach values to the outputs. In a democratic society these values are determined in the market place via dollars or in the political arena via votes. We may have some faulty voting practices—in the market as well as in politics—but this fact does not lead us to scrap this valuation mechanism.

We have the right to elect seemingly "inefficient" ways of doing things. If a man prefers to take a taxi rather than ride the subway, he can't be said to prefer an inefficient mode of transport. Likewise, a community may recognize the cost of maintaining its independence but yet be perfectly willing to bear it. What we cannot condone is the situation in which the costs to society at large are not adequately reflected in the prices confronted by the individual or the community in making its choice.

In the final analysis, therefore, metropolitan consolidation is mandatory only if there is no other way to deal with the external costs and benefits generated by autonomous decisions. But, before we can decide that issue, we need to go much farther than we have so far in identifying these spillovers. Until we do that, we would have a very inadequate foundation for managing a metropolitan government. And, after we have gone through this exercise, we might discover that it is perfectly feasible to negotiate compensation among communities rather than abandon the whole structure of local government.

PART I

Economic Structure and Growth

PITTSBURGH TAKES STOCK OF ITSELF
Edgar M. Hoover

*Dr. Edgar M. Hoover is Professor of Economics and Director of
the Center for Regional Economic Studies at the University of Pittsburgh. He has been associated with two of the most comprehensive
metropolitan studies: the New York Metropolitan Region Study
(1956-59) and the Pittsburgh Regional Economic Study (1959-62)
the latter of which he directed. His work in spatial economics dates
back to his doctoral dissertation—"The Theory of Location and the
Shoe and Leather Industries" (1933)—which is a classic in the field.*

*In this summary of the Pittsburgh study, Dr. Hoover develops a
major theme of our Introduction: how the structure of a region's
economy influences its growth.*

THE STUDY AND HOW IT DEVELOPED

The Pittsburgh Regional Planning Association has just published
the results of its Economic Study of the Pittsburgh Region—a
searching examination of the economy of one of the nation's oldest
and largest metropolitan industrial areas.

This project developed from serious postwar concern by Pittsburgh civic leaders about the health of their community. That concern, culminating in the Allegheny Conference on Community De-

Edgar M. Hoover, "Pittsburgh Takes Stock of Itself," *Pennsylvania Business
Survey* (January 1964), pp. 1-6. The Economic Study of the Pittsburgh Region,
summarized in this article, was conducted by the Pittsburgh Regional Planning
Association, with the author as study director and Dr. Benjamin Chinitz as associate director. Its reports are published by the University of Pittsburgh Press.
The three principal volumes, entitled *Region in Transition, Portrait of a Region,*
and *Region with a Future,* appeared in January 1964, a compact summary later
in the year. The area covered includes the six contiguous counties of Allegheny,
Armstrong, Beaver, Butler, Washington, and Westmoreland.

velopment, had already resulted in the widely known early achievements of the Pittsburgh renaissance. Fortunately, there was also in
the community the rare courage and insight to recognize that such
obviously needed face-lifting might not be enough, and that the
next moves on the economic front were not so obvious. Accordingly,
it was decided that while efforts would continue unabated for physical rehabilitation, industrial promotion, betterment of labor-manage-
ment relations, and improvement of higher educational facilities,
there would at the same time be launched a continuing diagnostic
effort in depth, upon the findings of which could be framed further
realistic programs directed at basic causes. . . .

THE BASIC DIAGNOSIS

What, then, did the study reveal about the Pittsburgh region?
The first objective was a thorough analysis of the economic structure. We looked especially for features that distinguished the region
from other American industrial areas, and for structural features
that presumably had some influence on growth prospects. We
sought to learn, also, how the present regional economic structure
had evolved out of the past, as a way to better understanding of
what might change it in future.

That first phase of the study yielded documentation of a host of
fairly obvious facts about the region's past and present. Since World
War I the Pittsburgh region has lagged increasingly behind the
growth trends not only of the United States as a whole but also
of the northeastern industrial heart of the United States. The region
has an unusually heavy burden of chronic unemployment, affecting
particularly the less skilled segments of the labor force. There is
a relative shortage of work opportunities for women in the region.
The industries which have been the traditional base of the regional
economy have ceased in the past few decades to provide a basis for
further regional employment growth.

None of the above findings will surprise anyone acquainted with
the region; but as the study's analysts dug deeper they brought to
light some less obvious features of the region's economy, suggestive

of the nature of the basic forces of growth and change. Net outward migration of people from the region, for example, was found to prevail not merely in the present and recent past, but at least as far back as 1920. It appears that the volume of the net outflow has increased in successive decades. The persistence of such an outflow, and the fact that it does not represent simply a cross section of the population but is heavily concentrated in white males of the younger working age groups, have affected the makeup of the region's population in terms of age, sex, and color. The outflow can in turn be explained in terms of trends in job opportunity as well as differences in mobility.

Further probing into the nature of the Pittsburgh region's industrial specialization likewise brought out some other important and not necessarily obvious facts. It appears that this region is exceptional both in terms of the intensity of its traditional specialization in a few industries and in terms of certain highly significant regional characteristics of plants, firms, occupations, and auxiliary services that this pattern of specialization has produced. Given the nature of the late nineteenth century coal-and-iron basis of Pittsburgh's industrial pre-eminence, it is no accident that the regional economy stands out from others in respect to large typical size of production units; large multiplant industrial corporations; a high proportion of male and of blue-collar jobs; a slightly lower average level of educational attainment; greater over-all instability of employment, income, and local business; a more restricted range of employment and entrepreneurial opportunities; and underrepresentation of nearly all types of independent business-service enterprises.

This probing into current facts and history gradually brought into focus a diagnostic picture of the regional economy. The Pittsburgh region faces a challenge of transition, which to date it has not fully succeeded in meeting. The pre-World War I basis of regional growth has been lost. This occurred partly because so much of Pittsburgh's earlier pre-eminence was based on specialization in industries which themselves are no longer expanding in terms of employment. It occurred mostly because such initial competitive strengths of the region as the strategic access advantage of location at the head of the

Ohio River, the local availability of high-grade coal, and a head start over midwestern centers in early development have all been vastly downgraded in importance by technological and market shifts.

But this raises a crucial question. Many other industrial regions have lost their original bases of pre-eminence, yet have managed to avoid general decline. They have been able to develop some new strengths and new activities to sustain growth. Why not Pittsburgh?

In a changing, dynamic economy, no specific regional specialization or strength can be relied upon to last forever. Pittsburgh itself has indeed some record of successful adjustment of this sort during the nineteenth century: some once fairly important industries in the area, such as textiles and clothing, oil refining, carriages, salt, and shipbuilding, have disappeared or greatly diminished in local prominence without any apparent lasting effect on over-all regional growth. The fact must be faced, in diagnosis and prognosis for the region, that this ability to roll with the punches has seemed somewhat inhibited in recent decades. The study throws a good deal of light on this apparent lack of resilience.

It can be explained in part by the sheer magnitude of the adjustment required. The Pittsburgh region was so heavily specialized in a narrow range of industries that, when these all at the same time ceased to provide further growth of employment for the region, an extremely fast pickup in other regional activities would have been required to take up the slack.

A second explanation can be found in the region's industrial assets —labor skills, business know-how, physical facilities, local supporting services, amenities, market connections, and so on. There is a very wide qualitative disparity between the kinds of assets developed for the area's traditional heavy-industry specialties and the kinds of assets required under each of these headings to make the region attractive to those industries that have accounted for most industrial growth since World War I.

Finally, flexible adjustment has been further impeded by some special rigidities or deficiencies stemming from the region's historical background of narrow specialization and slow growth. Physical facilities and urban layouts are older and more cramped than in areas with a more dynamic recent history, and thus in many cases more difficult to keep up to date. The area's manpower pool (including both employers and employees) is characterized by somewhat greater age and seniority in specific industry or occupational lines and can be presumed, by that token, to be somewhat less flexibly adaptable to change. The region, primarily by virtue of its specialization in types of industry involving very large plants and very large firms, has a notably smaller complement and variety of the kinds of supporting services upon which small and new firms are particularly dependent. The sources of venture capital and enterprise in an old industrial center like Pittsburgh, long wedded to mammoth enterprises of national or international scope, are not so easily available for starting up relatively small and novel types of business as they are in many other areas with a different history and structure. Giant corporations which for historical reasons have their headquarters in this region have in most instances no special incentive to locate within the Pittsburgh region their ventures into new fields of production as they or their predecessors did in the nineteenth century when capital and enterprise were less mobile and tended to seek outlets close at hand. After private fortunes have been built up on the basis of the industrial pioneering of previous generations, their heirs understandably are not always so eager as were the forebears to share the risks of staking untried local innovators. Moreover, there seems to be evidence that local public services have been adversely affected (in relation to cost) in both availability and quality.

THE REGION AND ITS PARTS

An important part of the study (covered in the second of the three published volumes, *Portrait of a Region*) concerned the changing relationships of the region's component areas. To avoid excessive length in this article, that part of the work will be noted here only in the most summary fashion.

The essential finding is that rapidly increasing internal interdependence among the various parts of the region makes the whole, in functional terms, more and more a regional entity and not just an arbitrarily delimited stretch of territory.

This increased interdependence is shown in many ways. More worker mobility and new geographical patterns of employment and residence have greatly increased the amount and range of commuting and other daily travel inside the region, and it is certainly far more legitimate now than formerly to conceive of a single regional "labor market." Centralized and large-scale administrative, service, and distribution activities play a more important role in the regional economy compared to the older pattern of neighborhood, town, or other subregional self-sufficiency that prevailed in pre-automobile days. Access to regional recreational and cultural facilities is more important for two reasons. Higher incomes and more leisure have made such activities more important relative to other lines of consumption and productive activity, and greater ease of travel has given the region's people access to such facilities all over the region rather than just in their own subareas. Exploding space requirements for productive activities have rapidly spread development from older centers to outlying areas and have made provision of adequate industrial and other sites a regional rather than a purely local concern.

More and more, then, the fortunes of each part of the region depend on the continued economic health of the region as a whole, and upon taking most advantage of the proximity of its parts.

OLD TRENDS AND NEW

Peering into the future, investigators turned first to appraising the directions in which the momentum of recent past trends and some discernible broad national economic growth trends would lead the region within the next twenty to twenty-five years. The provisional projections showed quite clearly the challenging transition character of the current stage of the region's economic history. The region seems to be at a parting of the ways. The inertial path of the trends leads forbiddingly downhill—not in the sense of actual shrinkage in employment, population, or income for the region, but in the sense of an even greater lag behind national growth trends that are widening the gap between growth of employment opportunity and the natural increase of population. A more acceptable outcome would seem to depend on breaking through onto a new path, developing new sources of growth.

That view was supported by the study's detailed analysis of prospects in the region's main basic industries: mining, primary metals, chemicals, glass, electrical machinery, and administrative and research activity. Though no contingency can be ruled out as altogether impossible, we cannot realistically look to mining, primary metals, chemicals, glass, or the types of electrical equipment in which the region is now specialized to take up any of the slack, at least on balance. These "traditional" regional specialties are much more likely, on the contrary, to decline somewhat further in their combined employment in the region and thus serve to widen the employment gap. Among the key activities studied in detail, administrative and research activity and the electronics and communications equipment sectors of the electrical machinery industry group are those with real regional growth prospects in any event and with an impressive potential under the most favorable circumstances.

STRENGTHS AND WEAKNESSES

A basic task of the study analysts was to identify what kinds of broad capabilities of access, physical facilities, manpower skills, organization, and community environment a region will need if it is to exploit the new opportunities as they come into view, and to ride the wave of technological progress and growth instead of succumbing to the undertow.

The Pittsburgh region has the important advantages of a large metropolitan labor market with the potential for diversity and flexibility that size itself implies, in addition to an impressive array of skills at the manual, technical, professional, and managerial levels. On the other hand, by comparison with a good many other urbanized areas of its size, it faces a more formidable problem of transition entailing the retooling and upgrading of its productive manpower and the filling of certain gaps that may widen before they are closed.

Access advantage was historically the major reason for Pittsburgh's start and early growth to major status among American urban and industrial areas, but that was a century ago. For a narrow range of bulk commodities, river transport connections are a significant regional asset. Probably of greater significance for the future is the central position of the region relative to the highly developed northeastern quadrant of the United States, but margins of access advantage among major Northeastern centers are rather small and diminishing in importance.

Even the region's hilly topography, which at first sight seems a serious developmental handicap and in the past has undoubtedly been just that, now offers increasing opportunities for exploitation as an asset. Both physical and cultural amenities in the region will most certainly assume far greater importance than at any time in the past as determinants of economic growth in addition to their direct welfare value.

The whole array of advantages implied by major metropolitan status is a most important element in the Pittsburgh region's potential for renewed impetus to growth and improvement. This is true partly because Pittsburgh already possesses many of the essentials for playing a large role as one of the nation's major regional capitals: geographic centrality and transport connections, large size, and a concentration of major business leadership and capital. It is true secondly because most of the kinds of employment that are growing most rapidly in this country are concentrated in sizable metropolitan areas. Finally, the region has an opportunity enhancement of its position in this respect precisely because it has been lagging in some ways in developing some truly "metropolitan" characteristics. For historical and structural reasons already set forth, the Pittsburgh region has never quite "grown up to its size" in the scope and quality of many types of business and public services, cultural and educational facilities, diversification of business, internal transport, and regional coordination of purpose and planning. In some of these respects, particularly the last, there are signs of a belated catching-up.

THE CHALLENGE

The study's projections indicate that the over-all employment problem of the region will remain at best as the overriding concern for many years, and that it may become even worse. It has to be approached, then, on a long-range basis; and corrective actions which might not have any real impact for several years cannot reasonably be dismissed on that score.

Holding the Line on Employment

In view of the deep-seated character of the region's economic maladjustment, as is manifested by the fact that it has become gradually more and more evident for at least forty years, even holding the line with current rates of unemployment and net out-migration would represent a substantial accomplishment, not to be assured without major continuing effort. The Pittsburgh renaissance, launched after World War II, has brought major accomplishments in downtown and industrial urban renewal, smoke control, river pollution abatement, expressway construction, and some vigorous industrial promotion and planning effort. Though the impact of these efforts is of course a continuing one, the region's economic performance in the postwar period would unquestionably have been much less adequate in the absence of those policies and actions. Yet that performance was unsatisfactory. This suggests that not merely continued but greatly intensified improvement effort will be required to make a real bite on the chronic unemployment problem over the long run. So far, the region has not fully demonstrated that it can hold the line.

Basic forces shaping the region's structure and growth can be objects of policy action, to the extent that they are amenable to action from within the region. Where they are not (as will often be the case), regional policy can seek only to promote the best adjustment to foreseeable changes. For example, the upgrading of the regional labor pool is a growth lever which can be pulled from inside the region; while the future trend of demand for steel pipe or flat glass is something to which the region can only adjust.

External Influences

To a considerable extent the region's economic future is conditioned by certain broad national shifts in population, markets, and industry that affect all regions. The West has been growing faster than the East for a long time and is likely to continue to do so for at least a few decades. The various parts of the country are tending to become more nearly alike, or at least less sharply different, in respect to population density, degree of industrialization, industrial structure, level of income, and characteristics of population. And within major urbanized regions an outward suburbanization of both residence and business continues. All these are basic trends, neither peculiar to nor originating within the region. Policy in the region, then, should not be directed toward either abetting or combating these trends, but toward adjustment to them—meeting the problems they raise and exploiting the opportunities they create. The broad shifts of population and markets, largely westward, coupled with the increasing importance of market access for industry location and the tendency for more and more parts of the country to achieve their own diversified industrial bases, has inevitably limited the role that this region, or any other, can play as a supplier of staple goods to nationwide markets.

The quickening stream of technological change represents another set of "outside" influences that profoundly affect the region but cannot be significantly affected from inside the region. Here again, the regional policy decisions can promote appropriate adjustment and utilization of new opportunities provided.

Rapid technological change means rapid obsolescence of physical facilities and skills alike. By that token it poses particularly serious adjustment problems to areas like the Pittsburgh region which have especially large proportions of their physical and human resources committed in terms of earlier technical conditions. Old industrial facilities are in general more expensive to keep up to date by piecemeal modernization, and the same holds true of old community layouts, public service facilities, and housing. Very much the same is true of human resources as well—the adaptability of workers and of business firms to new tasks and opportunities is less when a high proportion of those workers and firms have been doing substantially the same thing for a long time and have acquired a large stake in the status quo, and when there is a relative dearth of new and young entrants to the labor force and the business community who are prepared to take up new and unfamiliar functions.

There are several reasons why these problems of adapting both physical and human resources to changing needs in a region are much less likely to solve themselves in future and will call for more public planning and effort than in the past. One is the accelerated pace of technical change itself. A second is the fact that the amount of "investment" tied up in physical facilities and human capabilities is increasingly great, which makes adaptation and flexibility a greater challenge. A third reason, related to this last, is that higher technical standards narrow the range of types of work in which a person with no special skills at all can simply "learn by doing" or earn a living by manual labor. A fourth reason has to do specifically with interregional competition and will be explored below.

A century and a half ago Pittsburgh's geographic advantages in terms of position and natural transport routes were such that it would have been difficult to prevent its rise as one of America's principal commercial and industrial centers. In the latter nineteenth century, it would scarcely have been possible to prevent Pittsburgh from becoming one of the world's greatest centers of iron and steel production. The glass and coal-chemical industries, similarly, became important parts of the region's industrial foundation on the basis of strategic advantages of access or materials provided by nature.

Internal Influences

Nowadays, however—as has been documented over and over again in this study's findings—such factors of strategic transport advantage or availability of materials, fuels, and energy exert far less of a constraint. They apply to a smaller proportion of industrial activities, and the interregional differentials are narrower.

To a greater and greater extent, as a result, a region's success in

holding and attracting employment is determined by other locational considerations, most of which can be influenced from within
the region.

This radical change in the role of location factors poses for the
Pittsburgh region both its biggest economic problems and its biggest hope for the future. Most of the region's loss of pre-eminence
in its old industrial specialties is traceable to the weakening of once-
commanding advantages over other areas in transportation, fuel and
energy supply, and business capital and enterprise. But the new
kinds of advantage that will be decisive in the latter twentieth century are within the region's capability to generate on its own initiative. People rather than physical geography will play the leading
part in shaping the region's future.

GUIDELINES TO ACTION

Flexibility, modernity, and receptiveness to change are the key-
notes of policy here; and this is something that can be accomplished
in and by the region itself. This kind of policy could not possibly be
accomplished, in fact, in any other way. With respect to physical
facilities, much of the action indicated comes under the general
head of urban renewal. With respect to manpower resources, the
central task is an educational one. The labor resources of the region
can be made adaptable to a radically new and continually changing
set of demands and opportunities by (1) raising the standard of
basic education, (2) providing improved and broader technical
training for new entrants to the labor force, and (3) making it
feasible for those already in the labor force to retool their abilities.
The traditional notion of just one initial period of education in an
individual's lifetime, which equips him to "follow his trade" from
then on, is coming to be recognized as obsolete. During one person's working life of half a century, the kinds of work to be done
in our society change out of all recognition. Today's teen-ager will
have to acquire new skills, or whole new sets of skills, several times
before he retires, if he is to maintain status and income as a productive member of society.

Last, but by no means least, is a whole field of action involving improvement of the region's attractiveness as a place to live and work. Age and the traditional industrial complexion of the region, to say nothing of the largely outdated image of grime and obsolescence, are handicaps to be overcome in this regard. The Pittsburgh renaissance has already made impressive strides, and bright promise is shown by some further bold plans that are already beginning to be implemented in the downtown and Oakland areas and elsewhere. Higher living standards, more leisure, and greater population mobility make it increasingly important for any community to provide a far higher level of convenience, sightliness, public services, recreation, and cultural and educational opportunity than was ever before the case, and this trend will continue.

For the Pittsburgh region, the importance of improvement in this field is particularly great. The reason is that the Pittsburgh region's future depends to such a major extent upon retaining and attracting highly qualified and professional and technical people and business enterprisers, who are in demand everywhere and who command a high standard of residential amenity and cultural and professional opportunities.

Such are the areas within which it would seem that specific programs of action can most clearly work to cope with the challenges identified in this study. To achieve a better record than in the past will call for large investment of money and effort, and the assumption of risks inevitably associated with any investment that aims at a real breakthrough. It cannot be accomplished without a radically new degree of coordinated public and private action. What is involved here is a regional revitalization project for which there is no precedent among American urbanized areas.

LABOR MARKET PERSPECTIVES
OF THE NEW CITY

Arnold R. Weber

Arnold R. Weber, a professor at the University of Chicago Graduate School of Business, delivered a lecture at the University of Pittsburgh in a series entitled "Revitalizing the Old City." This lecture emphasized the role of the city in facilitating adjustment to changing supply-and-demand factors in the labor market, and suggested what must be done to enable the city to function in this role when faced by radically new circumstances.

The city has long been a gateway to individual economic opportunity. Ancient chronicles relate that young men journeyed from the outlying provinces of Rome in quest of their fortunes. Young women soon followed in search of the young men. As a mark of our advanced civilization, these objectives are no longer so boldly stated, but the process is essentially the same today as it was centuries ago. The Mississippi sharecropper rides a day coach on the Illinois Central, alternately known as the Freedom Road, because a relative wrote that the steel mills were hiring again. The college girl from Altoona joins a friend in New York to pursue what she hopes will be a mercifully brief career with an advertising agency. A hundred years' accumulation of grime has not dulled the promise of the city. The continued growth of urban centers in the United States, Europe, and now Africa attests to the universal economic attractions of the city. Although the weekend visitor may be diverted by museums and theaters, the aspirations and productive activities of the city's inhabitants still comprise the foundation stones upon which urban life is built.

In fact, the modern city and the modern labor market are con-

Arnold R. Weber, "Labor Market Perspectives of the New City," lecture delivered at the University of Pittsburgh, March 17, 1964.

temporaneous developments. Both arose in the wake of the Industrial Revolution and the subsequent establishment of centralized, large-scale production units. The new economic environment created an expanded demand for labor around the site of the factory. This demand was initially satisfied by drawing upon available manpower —or childpower—and eventually casting a net which reached far into the agricultural areas. In Lancashire, England, for example, the cottonmill owners first conscripted children from the local workhouses to man the new factories. They bolstered this juvenile work force with women and ultimately recruited new hands from as far away as Ireland and Wales. The availability of a specialized supply of labor, in turn, attracted additional firms to the area. Concurrently, the demand for labor was further augmented by enterprises serving the needs of the firms and workers that had come before. In this manner, the modern urban labor market arose both as a response to industrialization and as a stimulant to further economic growth. The process has been repeated with some variation in this country, although few observers would support the thesis that child labor is essential to economic growth.

Viewed in this manner, the local labor market is a crucial element in urban development, linking the city to the wider economic environment. As the technical and economic climate changes, new pressures will impinge on the city through the labor market. In this respect, a survey of current trends indicates that the urban labor market presently is undergoing a major transformation, placing a heavy burden on existing institutional arrangements for the use of human resources. In addition to dealing with traffic congestion and the recurrent demands of the local baseball team for a new stadium, the city fathers will also have to give conscious attention to the organization and operation of the labor market as such.

As in the past, recent changes in the urban labor market have reflected new methods of production. Many of these technological developments have been popularly identified with automation. Clearly, automation is to industrial engineering as sex was to psychology—that is, it has kindled the public's interest in a heretofore obscure branch of knowledge while giving rise to great fears of dire consequences if the practice is carried too far.

Broadly speaking, automation involves the substitution of machines for human effort and judgment in the implementation and control of production. In a chemical or paper plant it may mean the introduction of continuous process operations regulated by feedback control mechanisms. In a commercial bakery or coal mine, automation may involve the mechanization of materials-handling. In banks, insurance companies, and government agencies, the surge of new technology is signified by the computer, with its immense capacity for storing and manipulating great masses of information at high speeds.

Following the pattern of the earlier Industrial Revolution, these innovations have had a significant effect upon the demand for labor. Because the demand for labor is influenced by a host of variables, it is not always possible to isolate those changes that may be specifically related to automation alone. It is possible, however, to offer a few generalizations with some degree of confidence. First, it is undeniable that in specific situations technical change—i.e., automation—has resulted in a net reduction in employment. This consequence has been observed in particular plants in the meatpacking, oil refining, electronics, steel, coal, and paper industries. The magnitude of the reduction varies, of course, with the extent of the change, but in some cases it has exceeded 50 per cent. Paradoxically, these reductions in employment may not result in any direct unemployment, because the size of the work force is diminished by the so-called attrition approach: through deaths, resignations, and retirements. Nonetheless, there is a diminution of particular employment opportunities which no longer exist for new entrants into the labor market.

In many cases, the industries affected have been the primary source of employment in a given urban labor market. Thus, cities like Pittsburgh and Detroit are especially vulnerable to the employment effects of technical change because of the dominant position occupied by the steel and automobile industries in these labor markets. On the other hand, New York, Chicago, and St. Louis have a more diversified industrial mix and are less likely to feel the impact of automation when it makes deep inroads into a single industrial sector.

The Bureau of Labor Statistics has made one estimate of the effect of technological change on the entire manufacturing sector of the economy. Although fraught with statistical perils, this study indicated that approximately 200,000 jobs disappeared annually between 1953 and 1959 as a result of improved methods of production. Over-all, technical change has helped to keep total employment in the manufacturing sector at a relatively constant level since 1957 while output has increased by approximately 30 per cent. Moreover, employment has actually declined from 10 to 20 per cent in specific industries such as transportation equipment, steel, and petroleum. Even greater reductions in force were noted in the mining industry where prodigious increases in productivity have taken place during the postwar period. Those cities that have most of their labor market eggs in these industrial baskets have been confronted with major adjustments in labor demand. The pressures on the labor market are magnified when the effects of the decline of employment in the basic manufacturing or mining industries are transmitted to the secondary sectors.

Second, automation has been a powerful force contributing to changes in the structure of the labor force. Recent technological advances have dealt the heaviest blows to semiskilled operatives and industrial laborers—those groups that have long been the exemplification of blue-collar virtue in the urban labor market. At the same time, major gains have been registered in the number of professional and technical workers, mechanics, repairmen, and other occupational groups concerned with the development and maintenance of complex productive equipment. In the aggregate, automation has reinforced other trends in the economy which have undermined the dominance of blue-collar workers. By the middle 1950's, the labor force had crossed a Great Divide, and presently more people are employed in white-collar occupations than in blue-collar occupations.

Although the chain of causation becomes more tenuous, one additional consequence of technical change for the structure of employment warrants attention. In addition to affecting the level and occupational composition of employment opportunities, the new technology may also influence the geographical location of jobs. When a firm introduces a major technical change, it is likely to make other basic modifications, particularly those relating to the geographical location of facilities. This may mean the further erosion of the traditional employment base that has sustained the urban labor market. In the meatpacking industry, for example, shifts in population and changes in the marketing of livestock have diminished the economic attractions of historical centers of production such as Chicago and Kansas City. Thus when advanced technology was introduced, it was likely to be in a new plant situated in an area that met a broad range of economic requirements. Chauvinists in Vermont take a perverse pride in noting that that state has more cows than people. Similarly, Chicago may lay a claim to uniqueness by pointing out that currently more people than cows are killed annually within its borders.

Parallel developments have taken place in the automobile industry where, over the last decade, the introduction of new technology has accompanied the steady movement of production facilities away from Detroit. Akron's claim to pre-eminence in the production of rubber tires also has been long muted by the movement of tire and tube plants to other parts of the country. And any visitor to the Boston area will be shown the ruins of textile mills with a veneration normally associated with a trip to Bunker Hill.

When a major industry departs or dies, the instinctive reaction of the community is to seek suitable replacements. A perusal of the literature of local industrial development commissions clearly indicates that electronics is the all-purpose curative for urban economic ills. In any case, cities as diverse as Boston and Chicago have made strenuous efforts to transform meat-cleavers or looms into transistors. Smaller cities with greater vision have turned to ski lodges and artificial lakes. When a city succeeds in attracting new industry either to supplement or replace traditional enterprises, the arrival of these firms may have further consequences for the urban labor market. That is, such firms are likely to shun the central core of the city and instead, locate on its periphery or in the suburbs. In the past, the center of the city was the appropriate site for industry because of the proximity to a river or railroad freight yards or important sources of labor. Many of the new industries, however, do not have the same locational requirements. In view of the land costs associated with modern one-story factory and offices, the lure of the countryside is irresistible. Thus in Chicago there has been a pronounced shift of both new and old firms from the central city to the northwest suburbs. In Boston, the electronics industry sweeps around the city in a circumferential arch along Route 128. The movement of industry, along with the well-documented flights to the suburbs of residents seeking fresh air and low taxes—to be disillusioned in both cases—has also pulled service and trade employment with it. Within the typical American city, employment opportunities have moved away from the center core to areas that were lighted only by the twinkle in a real estate agent's eyes just a few years ago.

The consequences of these changes in labor demand have been intensified by equally portentous developments on the supply side of the labor market. Historically, the city has always been an important terminus for people seeking political freedom or the amelioration of their economic condition. The scope of this migration has been worldwide, as evidenced by the Jews in New York, the Irish in Boston, and the Poles in Pittsburgh. Despite the annoyance of the old residents, it is clear that this in-migration provided the sinews for the economic development of the typical, industrial American city. In effect, the urban labor market began at Ellis Island and extended westward to Chicago and Milwaukee.

With the passage of the National Origins Act of 1924, the flood of immigration from abroad was reduced to a trickle. Beginning around World War I, however, a different pattern of migration took shape that maintained a steady stream into the urban labor market. In growing numbers, Negroes left the rural backwash of the South for the nation's major industrial centers. If he did not look the same or speak the same language, the Negro responded to the same visions of political freedom and economic amelioration that had moved the Pole, the Irishman, and the Jew. The movement accelerated during the 1950's, when 1.5 million Southern Negroes followed the golden highways to the North and West.

This exodus generally has been from the farms to the cities. By

1960, 73 per cent of the Negro population was living in cities, compared to 70 per cent of the white population. One fifth of the total Negro population in the United States lives in a half-dozen Northern and Western cities: New York, Chicago, Philadelphia, Detroit, Washington, and Los Angeles. In the twenty-five largest cities in the country, the proportion of Negroes ranges from 55 per cent in Washington to 29 per cent in Detroit, 17 per cent in Pittsburgh, and 2.5 per cent in Minneapolis.

Although the vision that inspired this movement to the city was similar to that of the old migration, the reality has been harshly different. The Pole who came to Chicago or Pittsburgh was likely to find employment in a steel mill where his strong back and dedication to self-improvement were duly rewarded. Through work and frugality, he managed to educate his children, buy a home, and give some credence to Fourth of July oratory. The prospects confronting the Negro migrant from the South in 1964 are not as sanguine. Available evidence indicates that through the 1940's and 1950's the Negro enjoyed a substantial improvement in his occupational status and income as he entered into the well-worn channels of the urban labor market. This picture has radically changed over the past ten years. That is, the unskilled or semiskilled jobs that constituted the primary ports of entry into the urban labor market have been diminishing as a result of technical change and the redeployment of industry. Thus at the same time that the magnitude of Negro migration to the industrial centers of the North and West has been increasing, the demand for labor has been reduced in those job categories for which the in-migrants are best equipped.

This sequence of labor market events for the recent in-migrant is described in a study of the experience of 330 recipients of public aid in Chicago. The group was comprised almost exclusively of Negroes, most of whom had come to Chicago from Mississippi in the late 1940's or early 1950's. Upon their arrival in the city, they usually obtained jobs as laborers in construction or heavy manufacturing. Over a period of years, many of these workers changed jobs and advanced to semiskilled occupations in the manufacturing sector. This climb up the economic ladder was cut short by the recession of 1957-58. Most of the subjects were laid off and were never recalled to their former jobs. Some succeeded in obtaining subsequent employment with marginal firms or short-term positions in the service industries. But these jobs proved to be only a waystation on the continued slide into chronic unemployment and dependence on public generosity. Doubtless this profile of economic rise and decline has been duplicated in many other urban centers. Suffering from severe deficiencies in education, these new members of the urban labor force have not been able to penetrate the promised land of white-collar and professional employment. Consequently, the relative advance of the Negro population in terms of employment and income has slowed perceptibly since 1955. Although only fragmentary data are available, the new white resident with related deficiencies has experienced similar disillusionment.

The quest for employment by the jobless has been made more difficult by the geographical dispersion of job opportunities over the metropolitan labor market. That is, the in-migrant or impoverished market participant—both white and Negro—is likely to occupy the older residential areas, located around the central city from which previous generations of workers walked to the mill or rode the trolley to the packinghouse. However, the movement of industry out of the central city has weakened the physical link between the job-seeker's place of residence and prospective places of work. This development has two consequences for the supply side of the labor market. First, the traditional channels of the labor market information are no longer as effective as they were in the past. Almost all labor market studies indicate that the favored methods of seeking employment are consultation with friends and neighbors and direct application at the plant gate. Where the neighbors themselves are unemployed and the plants are dispersed over a wide area far from the job-seeker's place of residence, these techniques of search are not likely to be fruitful. Many of the jobs that are available can only be identified through information channels that generally are not operative in the central city.

Second, those who do succeed in finding employment may have to pay a price in terms of substantial transportation costs, both in time and money. In the past, commuting to work was associated with corporate presidents and bankers. As part of our continued progress in democracy, commuting is now a privilege extended equally to domestic servants and janitors. Many of the unskilled and semi-skilled job-holders currently journey from their places of residence near the center of the city to places of employment around the periphery of the metropolitan labor market. This pattern of "reverse commuting" has been noted in most major urban labor markets. Another Chicago study revealed, for example, that Negro workers, on the average, travel about twice as far to work as their white counterparts. This difference in distance traveled, it may be further noted, is not reflected in wage differentials. Moreover, Negroes who seek to cut this cost by moving closer to their places of work are frequently thwarted by discriminatory practices in the real estate market. Thus a new class has emerged in the urban labor market. Its members are separated from the mainstream of economic activity by deficiencies in skill and education, pronounced gaps in the labor market information system, and increased physical distance.

The problems posed by these changes in the organization of the urban labor market are not likely to be dissipated by the passage of time. Indeed, it would be difficult for Doctor Pangloss—or even Casey Stengel—to retain equanimity in the face of current labor force trends. During the decade of the 1960's, the United States will experience the largest increase in the work force for any ten-year period in history, when 26 million new young workers enter the labor market. Even with the attrition of people presently working, the nation's labor force will grow by 13 million. Nearly half of this net increase will be comprised of persons under twenty-five years old.

To put these developments in another way, while the total labor force is expanding by 17 per cent, the number of young people in the labor force will be increasing by 45 per cent. In 1960 there were 13.7 million young men and women working or seeking work; in 1970 this figure will be about 20 million. In contrast, in 1960 there were only 400,000 more young people in the labor force than ten years before. Again, much of the impact in this increase in the size of the labor force will be felt in the urban labor market.

In the past, the city and its labor market have been the beneficiaries of economic progress and the mass movement of people. Today these same factors have underscored that old economic maxim that you never get something for nothing. That is, they have thrust upon the cities the burden of accommodating the major changes besetting the nation today. It is clear that the immediate problem of adjustment involves the employment status of young workers and members of minority groups, primarily Negroes. It is now almost platitudinous to point out that the unemployment rate for Negroes is double the rate for white workers, as uninspiring as the latter may be. The inferior economic position of Negroes extends to virtually every occupational class, from craftsmen and foremen to industrial laborers. More ominously, the contraction of economic opportunities for Negroes has resulted in a withdrawal from the labor market and apathetic idleness. Thus in 1948 only 5.3 per cent of Negro males between twenty-five and sixty-four years of age were not actively seeking work; in 1963 this figure had risen to 8.2 per cent—again, nearly double the equivalent rate for white male workers. In some cases the increased economic idleness of Negro males is compensated by the increased labor market participation of women who have taken jobs in the low-wage service and light manufacturing industries. In some cities such as Pittsburgh, however, the industry mix and the apparent durability of the old-fashioned ideas about male dominance have not made female employment an easy substitute for male unemployment.

Obviously, the changing nature of the urban labor market has helped to fire the current "civil rights revolution." The Negroes' drive for economic and social equality probably owes as much to automation as to Dr. Martin Luther King. Aside from the matter of moral principle, which was dutifully obscured for one hundred years, the narrowing range of economic opportunities within which most Negroes now operate makes the call for militant action strident and irresistible.

A similar urgency prevails when examining the labor market status of young workers. Even in relatively good times, the unemployment rate of teen-age workers has exceeded 15 per cent of this age group. For high school dropouts, special studies by the Department of Labor have indicated that the unemployment rate in this age group is as high as 27 per cent. Other, closer investigations of census tracts in the Negro sections of Detroit have shown that the combined effect of age, limited education, and race may cause the unemployment rate to spiral as high as 50 per cent near the central city. The gravity of the problem of providing some immediate economic activity for new entrants into the labor market is underscored by data concerning labor force attachment. In 1953, the last time full employment was attained in the American economy, those with no previous work experience comprised only 4.4 per cent of the total unemployed. By 1958, this figure had risen to 9.3 per cent and in 1963 it reached a high of 14.8 per cent. Thus approximately one out of seven of those seeking work had yet to experience their economic baptism in the labor market.

The long-run problems of urban labor markets pose equally demanding challenges. The city can no longer depend upon the continued in-migration of green hands to satisfy its manpower requirements in an age of automation. Instead, it must allocate an increased proportion of its resources to developing the skills that are required by the new technology and industrial distribution of employment opportunities. A reliance on simple mobility, in fact, will probably accentuate the problem. As already indicated, the mass of in-migrants normally does not offer the skills required by the modern labor market. Similarly, as economic opportunities contract in an urban area, the higher-quality labor is likely to depart for greener fields. In West Virginia, it is sometimes said that every time a baby is born another college man leaves the state. Thus, those who are left are likely to be of lower quality or past the prime of their working lives.

As any medical doctor can tell you, it is easy to be long on diagnosis and short on remedial prescription, although these distinctions are seldom recognized in his fees. At any rate, the limits of this presentation do not permit an exhaustive treatment of the various programs that have or may be proposed to deal with the current problems of these urban labor markets. It is possible, however, to indicate broadly the direction and form that such policies may take.

Essentially there are three ways by which the urban labor market may be adapted to the new set of conditions: by influencing the demand for labor, by upgrading the supply of labor, or by improving the organization and operation of the market. The first approach—influencing the demand for labor—is generally beyond the autonomous efforts of city officials. Although a small town in southern Illinois may proclaim the beginning of an era of community growth with the opening of a new shoe plant, such triumphs are of small consequence in a large urban center. Instead, the maintenance of a high level of aggregate demand within the large cities is primarily a function of market factors and national economic growth. Without this growth and a continued expansion of employment opportunities, no fundamental solutions can be achieved even if all prospective job seekers are white, thirty years old, and have doctoral degrees in solid state physics. The appropriate policies for the attainment of the necessary rate of growth constitute a complex technical subject that will be given only this scant consideration. The best thing city-dwellers can do in this area is to vote for congressmen who do not think that Keynes's *General Theory* is the text of the devil.

If local policies are to have some determinate effect upon the operation of the urban labor market, they must focus on the supply of labor and the organization of the market. Although both of these elements will also be influenced by regional and national developments, they are directly responsive to local efforts. Four types of measures may be suggested that bear on these aspects of the market.

First, it is essential that young persons and the chronically unemployed maintain some connection with useful economic activity. Too often, the lack of immediate employment opportunities has resulted in a withdrawal from the labor market and continued dependence on public aid. At the risk of raising the ire of the social workers, work relief rather than the passive receipt of welfare funds should be considered as a realistic policy alternative. In addition, the city may provide employment opportunities on a subsidized basis in "sheltered industries," such as hospitals and utilities which are normally removed from competitive pressures in the product market. Other steps may be taken by private businesses and unions to offer gainful economic activity to the young and the unemployed. Pilot projects on both a public and private basis have been initiated in Chicago, New York, and St. Louis, among others. In Chicago, the Department of Public Aid has underwritten an expanded program for the "work habituation" and placement of public welfare recipients. This program, which uses the threat of loss of welfare benefits as a goad, has been marked with some success. None of the participants in the program have yet joined the local country club, but many hard-core unemployed workers have renewed their contact with the labor market and the discipline of work.

Second, the retention of some contact with the labor market can only have a salutary effect in the long run if it is supported by greatly expanded investment in basic and vocational education. Vocational education in the United States has long had an anachronistic quality, signified by breadboards and plowshares. The basic legislation for federal support of vocational education is the Smith-Hughes Act of 1917. Under this act, more than half of the $48 million appropriated for vocational education annually is earmarked for the support of training in home economics and agricultural occupations. With a fine sense of irony, this distribution of funds runs directly counter to current labor force trends. In 1950, approximately 15 per cent of the labor force was engaged in agricultural occupations; in 1960 only 8.5 per cent of the nation's work force remained on the farm.

Although some of my best friends are farmers or home economists, the character of current labor demand puts a greater premium on white-collar and technical occupations than these symbols of nineteenth-century independence. Through substantial investment in vocational education, it may be possible to equip the new entrants into the labor force with the skills that are currently in demand and provide displaced workers with a new occupational foothold in the market. Moreover, the availability of adequate vocational education facilities gives the community the capacity to adapt its work force to the changing requirements of new industry. In Milwaukee and Fort Worth, for example, the existence of a progressive vocational education system has played an important role in maintaining the economic health of these cities.

One caveat may be entered concerning the administration of vocational education. That is, in the past craft unions have often exercised a proprietary interest over the conduct of vocational training in the skilled occupations. To be sure, trade unions can and do exercise a beneficial influence on vocational training, but too frequently this solicitude also reflects a desire to control entry into the bountiful sectors of the labor market. Aesop long ago warned us of the dangers of sending the fox to guard the chickens. Thus the administration and control of an expanded vocational education program should be broadly representative of the different groups in the community to prevent any single vested interest from claiming it as its special preserve.

Vocational education is, of course, an expensive proposition. However, if the choice is between expanded welfare payments or electronic instruments, the choice should surely lie with the latter. In this respect, some of the burden on the local community should be lifted by recent federal legislation signaling a massive commitment to occupational training. The Manpower Development and Training Act of 1962 and the Vocational Education Act of 1963 call for the allocation of billions of dollars for vocational education in one form or another over the next five years.

Third, training and vocational education, by itself, will not do the job in the modern labor market. Concerted attention must also be given to the collection and dissemination of labor market information. New channels of information will have to augment the traditional reliance on informal sources. In a complex labor market, the points of access to specific opportunities are more formal and limited and the problem of making a rational occupational choice can be formidable. Information is required about the present availability of jobs, hiring standards, techniques of job-seeking, and patterns of occupational progression. This information should be accompanied by the intensive counseling of new entrants into the labor market and those who are forced to acquire a new occupational orientation. These resources are not likely to be forthcoming from friends and relatives, especially if they have also experienced prolonged periods of unemployment.

The consequences of inadequate counseling and labor market information were vividly revealed by one study of five occupational retraining programs for unemployed workers. This study indicated that those trained for the more skilled occupations generally had a lower employment rate than those trained for lesser skills. In addition, the skilled trainees who found work were likely to be employed in jobs that were unrelated to their training. In a large measure, these disappointing results reflected the fact that many of the skilled trainees were forced to operate in alien sectors of the labor markets where they had little appreciation of the effective techniques of job-hunting.

At first glance, the local office of the state employment service appears to be the logical agency to carry out this task. In fact, the employment service has done much useful work in this area. Unfortunately, it is a fact of life that the employment service has never been fully accepted by many employers who reject the suggestion of dealing with the "unemployment office." The task of organizing the collection and dissemination of information in the labor market will have to be supplemented to a significant degree by municipal and private agencies that can enlist the support of large numbers of employers. Clearly, here is an opportunity for the personnel manager to translate his membership on the board of directors of the United Fund into a more concrete demonstration of interest in his community.

Fourth, the urban labor market can function effectively only if discriminatory barriers in housing and employment aimed at members of minority groups are overturned. The question of open occupancy is, of course, a controversial issue that touches upon many aspects of city living. There is little doubt, however, that segregated residential patterns impair the effective operation of labor markets. By eliminating such practices, there can be a broader diffusion of information and more extensive patterns of search by job-seekers in all sectors of the labor market. Consequently, members of minority groups may bid for job opportunities, especially those on the periphery of the urban labor market, from which they were previously foreclosed by ignorance or inordinate transportation costs. The gains for the city as a whole may be calculated in terms of the improved allocation of its human resources.

The necessity for nondiscriminatory hiring standards is obvious and needs no elaboration here. It has been said that there are more Negro college graduates driving buses in Chicago or sorting mail in the Atlanta post office than are employed by all the major corporations in the United States. Regardless of the literal accuracy of this statement, it highlights the economic waste and personal frustration resulting from discriminatory practices in the labor market. The rash of demonstrations in Northern cities in the past year serves notice that, one way or the other, the barriers will soon come tumbling down.

None of these measures, individually or collectively, offers an easy solution to the problems that currently beset the urban labor market. They merely add to the endless agenda of unfinished business that commands the attention of professors, politicians, and other overworked citizens of the great urban centers that dominate the American scene today. Those who would throw up their hands in despair and flee will probably find another city at the end of the road. For better or worse, most of the promise and burdens of modern society are found in the city. Over the course of history, the cities have survived and, indeed, flourished by passive adaptation to new circumstances. It would be best, however, if we met the present-day challenges of the urban labor market on our own terms rather than by having solutions thrust upon us by forces that we no longer control.

PART II

Urban Transportation Problems

KNOCKING DOWN THE STRAW MEN

John R. Meyer

Improving urban transit facilities, despite popular notions to the contrary, is only an indirect and excessively expensive way of solving the problems of our large cities. In addition, such improvement would hardly arrest the continuing shift of people, businesses, and employment opportunities to the suburbs. John R. Meyer, Professor of Economics at Harvard University, attributes the change in the nation's population pattern to more fundamental forces at work within our rapidly changing industrial society. The views expressed, which are solely the author's, grew out of research done for the Rand Corporation's Urban Transportation Study under a grant from the Ford Foundation.

It has become quite fashionable to worry about the present state and future possibilities of American cities which are allegedly sick and decaying. These developments, so the argument runs, are a cause for deep concern because Americans are increasingly an urban people, and large urban concentrations are essential to the maintenance of our cultural and aesthetic values. And finally, say the critics, the condition of our urban centers is in sharp contrast to the vitality and growth of low-density suburbs filled with single-family, mass-produced dwellings—deprecatingly referred to as "urban sprawl."

The sources of these "urban anxieties" are many. They have a hard, substantial basis in the fact that populations within the incorporated limits of most large cities have either declined or remained stable in the past decade while populations just outside of

John R. Meyer, "Knocking Down the Straw Men," reprinted from *Challenge, The Magazine of Economic Affairs,* a publication of the Institute of Economic Affairs, New York University (December 1962), pp. 7-11.

these limits, in suburbia and exurbia, have often grown phenomenally. There has also been a tendency for the wealthier segments of society to migrate outward to a greater degree than the poor.

This outmigration has been followed by a dispersal of retailing, with the result that the older central business districts have become relatively and often absolutely less important as commercial centers. Less obviously, but just as surely, industry has also been relocating from central to suburban locations.

Loss of both higher-income groups and commerce and industry usually means, of course, an erosion of city tax bases. This is occurring, moreover, at a time when city responsibilities as centers of urban regions may be rising since the rapidly growing suburbs contribute to a heavy increase in the total population and urban amenity requirements of most metropolitan areas. These population and income shifts also often increase, quite inequitably, central city shares of total welfare burdens in metropolitan areas. Obviously, many of these inequities are a result of archaic political institutions and boundaries that do not reflect present-day realities.

Unfavorable patterns of urban change are often blamed on the prevalence of the private automobile. In some city-planning circles the automobile has almost become an emotional symbol of all that is wrong with American cities. Not only is the automobile seen as the cause of much of the deplored decentralization, but it ostensibly has been aided and abetted in its wayward ways by unfortunate government policies that implicitly or explicitly subsidize overuse of automobiles. Among the many unfortunate results attributed to this "folly" is a decline in public transit services, often to the point of bankruptcy and abandonment.

At best, public transit reputedly is reduced to such a precarious financial state that it cannot find the money needed to develop new services in the areas of heavy population growth, thus giving residents in such areas no other option than traveling by car. The resulting rush of cars into downtown areas is said to be "strangling our cities," subjecting the public to a great health hazard by poisoning the air with noxious fumes, gobbling up precious urban land for "unproductive" automobile use, and, in general, ruining and debilitating our cities.

The usual proposal for correcting this ostensible mess into which urban transportation has fallen is to grant subsidies to public transit to compensate for the subsidies allegedly being given to urban auto-users. These subsidies would be used to restore services and otherwise improve the quality of public transit to the point where automobile-users would find it attractive to abandon their cars. It is often suggested that this subsidy money could be put to the best use by developing and extending rail rapid transit because this type of transportation can attain higher maximum operating speeds more quickly than any alternative and because it is "obviously cheaper" than other forms of urban transit.

Thus, at the moment, new rail rapid transit systems or extensions of existing systems are either being proposed or are under consideration in, among other places, Los Angeles, San Francisco, Atlanta, Cleveland, Washington, Boston, Philadelphia.

It is also often alleged that the revival of good public transit, especially of a rail variety, will have many favorable side effects. It will help arrest urban decentralization, maintain downtown property values, and create higher property values along its right of way. In general, the availability or unavailability of rapid transit is often pictured as a prime determinant of urban land-use and development patterns.

Sorting fact from fiction in all of this is very difficult, mainly because the two are so evenly balanced and thoroughly intermingled. There is no denying, for example, that some relative decentralization has apparently taken place in urban areas, but it is difficult to define and assess quantitatively the importance of the various factors contributing to this development.

It is clear, though, that the availability of public transit is just one of many factors contributing to decentralization. For example, many industries moved to less centralized locations because they needed large tracts of unencumbered land to properly set up efficient one-story manufacturing layouts. Also, the development of trucking, piggybacking, and other new techniques of moving freight from city to city no longer makes a location near a railroad marshaling yard necessary to receive either low-cost or high-quality freight service. The extremely low freight transport requirements of several important modern industries such as electronics, aircraft, and motion picture manufacture, to cite only a few, have further contributed to decentralization.

Furthermore, the increasing substitution of trucks for railroad freight cars as well as the increasing use of airlines instead of railroads for passenger transportation have moved employment opportunities in intercity transportation away from the central city.

In addition, bookkeeping industries like insurance are no longer as dependent on central locations and access to public transportation as a means of recruiting a low-salaried, unskilled female labor force. The existence of both cheap private transportation and electronic computers has made location far less important for these activities.

Similarly, a move to a suburban shopping center may not only provide a retailer with an opportunity "to get closer to his customers." It may, in addition, give him a chance to redesign his store structure from the ground up and thus enable him to incorporate a number of economies, particularly in freight handling and warehousing, that are impossible or difficult to introduce in an older building with a more constricted downtown location. Indeed, some suburban shopping centers have been created in advance of local residential demand in their vicinity.

A decentralization of employment opportunities is crucial because it permits a decentralization of residences without incurring any increase in commuter travel time or costs. As a consequence, a diffusion of employment locations can be enough to reduce urban population densities in and of itself. Reinforced by and interacting with increased ownership of private automobiles and higher personal incomes that permit wider ownership of single-family dwellings, the pressures for decentralization can be very nearly undeniable, regardless of what form of public transit may be available.

In the same vein, there is very little evidence that the presence of rail rapid transit tends to centralize employment opportunities or retailing, or that a dependence on highways leads to decentralization. . . . Central business districts and central cities have both prospered and languished with and without rapid transit. Furthermore, the presence of rapid transit provides no major barrier to the general tendency toward decentralization of employment opportunities in American cities.

The dispersion of employment opportunities also has a significant impact on the pattern of urban travel. One simple way of describing this change is to say that the pattern becomes characterized more by a large number of relatively uniform, low-level, and crisscrossing trip densities than by very high concentrations in a few corridors emanating like spokes from the center of the city, as was previously the case.

Among other things, the emergence of this crisscross travel pattern and its accompanying reduction in the density of trip demands makes it harder to design a satisfactory public transit system and alters the cost comparisons between different modes of public transit, as well as between public and private transport.

In general, an efficient public transit system is easier to design for a high density of demand than for a low density. This basic truth is strongly illustrated by the fact that even most existing or proposed rapid transit systems depend on automobiles and buses to conduce feeder operations from residential areas where population densities are low.

In fact, an integral part of most new transit proposals is the provision of extensive parking facilities at transfer points in the suburbs. A similar reliance on surface vehicles, usually buses, also characterizes most sensible plans for performing the collection and distribution function in central business districts. It is usually very inefficient to use high-performance line-haul vehicles, whether trains or buses, to perform downtown feeder functions because of the number of stops required.

It is often said that the chief advantage of railroad transit, particularly on highly traveled lines, is its low cost. The usual assertions of cost superiority for rail are based on the simple notion that rail can move 40,000 or more people per hour over a given stretch of right of way for less money than any alternative form of transport. Even granted that this is true, which it very well may not be, such an assertion is essentially irrelevant because rarely are demands of 40,000 persons per hour ever encountered in public transit operations, New York City being the one notable exception.

Additional perspective on the crucial demand-density problem can be obtained by [considering] the approximate number of persons leaving the central business districts of major United States cities during the evening peak hours. . . . The evening peak is particularly relevant because it usually exceeds the morning peak and represents the maximum demand placed on an urban transportation system.

[Of outstanding interest] is the magnitude of New York's peak volume [more than 800,000 commuters per hour leaving the central business district] over the two next largest cities [Chicago: 200,000-250,000, and Philadelphia: 150,000-200,000] and the relatively modest level of peak-hour volumes in most United States cities.

Translated into capacity requirements, 250,000 persons per hour can be accommodated easily in buses using only ten lanes of street or highway and 150,000 by using six lanes. Private autos with an average of only 1.5 people in each car would require about forty lanes to handle 100,000 per hour, twenty lanes for 50,000, and so on. Assuming only two lanes of usable outgoing capacity to a street, five highways would be required to handle a 250,000 volume level in buses and twenty exit streets and highways would be needed for 100,000 persons in private autos.

Of course, traffic would rarely move by only one mode. Assuming for illustrative purposes that half of the commuters could be induced to travel by transit bus while the rest went by auto, approximately nine or ten lanes would be required to move 50,000 people per hour, twenty lanes for 100,000, and so on. Although twenty lanes is a considerable highway capacity, it is not beyond that presently or about to be available in most U.S. cities. The only cities, moreover, with a peak rush-hour demand over 100,000 that are not *already* equipped with rail rapid transit are San Francisco and Los Angeles, which also happen to have two of the more extensive systems of limited-access urban highways.

Finally, it should be noted that the fragmentary data that are available on recent changes in peak-hour levels suggest that these are declining slightly, reflecting the tendencies toward decentralization mentioned earlier. In general, the aggregate level of demand for urban transportation, even during peak periods, would seem to be within manageable proportions in all but the largest cities and should become more manageable in the future.

For travel purposes other than commuting, both cost and service considerations have led to an increasing substitution of the private automobile for public transit. The auto's relatively low off-peak marginal cost, schedule flexibility, privacy, comfort, and cargo-carrying capacity have all combined to make it the dominant mode of transportation for shopping, personal business, social and recreational trips. Since these trips tend to occur mainly in noncommuter hours, loss of this business has tended to intensify the off-peak excess-capacity problem of public transit systems and created a loss in revenue unaccompanied by any significant cost reduction.

Indeed, the increased specialization of public transit in trips to and from work is a major source of many a transit system's financial problems. One possible solution to these problems, of course, would be to increase sharply prices charged to peak-hour users. Such a policy, however, is usually considered "politically impossible," and since public transit is usually either government-owned or regulated, these political considerations normally prevail.

Much the same conflict between economic and political reality also occurs in the pricing of highway facilities. For example, although there is little evidence that urban highway users are subsidized in the aggregate (in fact, urban contributions to highway and fuel taxes usually exceed expenditure), it seems highly probable that vehicles using high-cost central arteries and streets during peak periods are not paying their full costs. Again, rather than granting compensating subsidies to competing forms of transport, the economically rational solution would be to charge more for the use of these special facilities during rush hours; but such a solution is also considered politically impossible.

Because of the political obstacles, various alternatives to raising the cost of using these facilities have been suggested or actually put into use on urban highways. The search for an effective rationing device for urban highways during peak hours is highly important since, if it is granted that urban highways must be constructed to meet off-peak social, recreational, and shopping-trip demands, then the least expensive solution to the urban transportation problem is to find a way to make these same highways serve commuter needs. A fairly common suggestion has been to reserve lanes on freeways and streets for exclusive bus use during peak hours. Highways built exclusively for bus use also have been recommended.

Both of these plans, however, involve at least some probable underutilization of capacity since the lanes reserved exclusively for buses would either be inadequate for meeting peak demands or would be in excess supply during all other periods. Such excess capacity could be costly, moreover, if it occurred on limited-access facilities.

A preferable alternative, therefore, would be to combine priority access for buses with metering and control of access to high-performance urban expressways. Highway use would be limited to levels that permitted operation at high speeds and prevented traffic jams. Giving buses priority of access to these superior facilities would permit bus operations at high speeds without reserving lanes for exclusive bus use. The automobile commuter might also benefit since the elimination of traffic jams should increase the effective peak-hour carrying capacity of expressways for all purposes.

This metered-flow, priority-access idea is not only inexpensive to implement, but, like reserved lanes and special busways, does not involve a large investment in facilities that have no major alternative use, a weakness of rail transit investments.

A number of other policies might be instituted to effectuate relatively quick improvements in the availability of urban highway capacity during rush hours. Greater use of reversible lanes is one of the more obvious. Early completion of inner-belt and other circumferential highways often would prove helpful since a very high percentage of downtown rush hour traffic is commonly attributable to through traffic.

The development of more efficient urban transport also would be facilitated by the elimination of many archaic franchise regulations that restrict entry into taxi and bus operations. Most of these regulations serve no useful public purpose under modern conditions, their main effect being to create artificial property values for existing franchise-holders. These controls inhibit experimentation with new forms of urban transport and thereby create a rigidity that is most undesirable during a time of rapid change.

At present, the urban commuter usually has little range of consumer choice since he is essentially restricted to using either a rather inferior mass transit or an expensive and reasonably high-quality private auto service. It would seem highly probable that considerable potential exists for other services between these two extremes.

In sum, a number of simple, inexpensive policies exist which could eliminate much of the so-called urban transportation problem in most U.S. cities. Only New York, with its very special scale and complexity, might require drastic action. At a minimum, the available simpler remedies should be tested before large investments are made in expensive rail transit systems, the reputed advantages of which are doubtful at best.

Indeed, all transportation solutions to urban problems must be recognized as rather indirect attacks on the basic difficulties of poor land-use patterns, declining populations and tax bases, and unequal sharing of public burdens. By contrast, federally aided urban renewal, metropolitan governments, and more state aid to urban areas are all more direct ways of meeting these problems.

Since the resources available for meeting urgent urban problems are scarce, it seems foolish to undertake highly expensive, quixotic transportation programs of unproven effectiveness.

PART III

Planning in the Metropolitan Area

THE MYTH AND REALITY OF OUR URBAN PROBLEMS

Raymond Vernon

Dr. Vernon, currently Professor of International Finance at the Harvard Business School and Director of Harvard's Development Advisory Service, gained his experience in urban economics as Director of the New York Metropolitan Region Study. In that effort, Dr. Vernon and his staff confined their attention to diagnosis and prognosis. The object of these lectures, as Dr. Vernon puts it, is "prescription, not prognosis. . . . Personal values and personal perspectives are deeply involved."

If a major object of our existence were to create great cities of beauty and grace, there would be something to be said in favor of dictatorship. As a rule, the great cities of the past have been the cities of the powerful city-states in which a dominant king or governing body had the power and the will to impose its land-use strictures upon an obedient populace. Weak or divided local governments, responsive to the push and pressure of the heterogeneous interest groups which make up a city, have rarely managed to intervene enough to prevent the unpalatable kind of growth which typifies our larger American urban areas.

Up to a few decades ago, there was no serious effort by any American city to take a hand in shaping its development. Such efforts in the United States date back to the year 1916 when New York City put America's first comprehensive zoning law on its statute books. By that time, an elite group of New Yorkers could already see the outlines of some of their emerging problems. Land

Raymond Vernon, "The Myth and Reality of Our Urban Problems," from The Stafford Little Lectures of 1961, Joint Center for Urban Studies, Cambridge, Massachusetts (1962), pp. 33-47.

in downtown New York was being used incongruously and waste-
fully. Fish markets and ancient warehouses stood side by side with
temples of finance and giant office buildings. Tiny streets, built for
another age, were being choked with traffic and darkened by tower-
ing skyscrapers.

The problem was not solely that of downtown land use, however.
Real estate taxes were growing, seemingly without a limit. Besides,
the difficulties of daily ingress to the shops and offices of the central
business district were now beginning to appear as more and more
citizens moved off Manhattan Island into the distant reaches of
Brooklyn, the Bronx, and New Jersey. And in the other great cities
of the country, similar developments were also beginning to take
visible shape.

Something had to be done to arrest the deterioration of the community. The closest approximation to the peremptory powers of the
ancient kings was land-use planning, planning achieved through
the use of zoning ordinances. So the first pioneering steps were
taken.

It should not go unnoticed that the strongest support came from
a part of the community which the casual observer might have considered least ready for it—the merchants, the financiers, and the
daily press, whose ideology seemed almost unqualifiedly committed
to the proposition that the interference of government in the economic affairs of men was unwise and unproductive. The reasons
for which these groups were the first to rise in support of so drastic
a use of the police power, however, will already be clear to my
readers. These groups more than any others—partly because of
sentiment, partly because of offended values, partly because of
self-interest—had the strongest stakes in changing the course of the
urban areas' development pattern.

The wisdom of some kind of land-use planning, however, was also
apparent to many groups outside the central business district. Many
communities were beginning to appreciate that when abattoirs sat
alongside high-priced houses, neither benefited from the contact.
When an industrial area blocked access to a residential neighborhood, both were hurt by the propinquity. When enclaves of land
were spoiled by nearby uses, and remained unused, neglected, and

overlaid with weeds and trash, no one gained from the loss of precious space. Community after community, therefore, acquired the legal power to regulate the use of land, until today most of our urban areas are blanketed by a patchquilt of land-use regulations.

But there was slippage, considerable slippage, between the abstract concepts that justified land-use planning and the actual practice of the art. In the older sprawling cities of America, the zoning tool had come too late to have much effect on the style and pattern of urban life. Most of the land of the downtown areas was already covered with structures whose uses were largely fixed until the time when there would be some economic reason for razing the buildings and beginning all over again. And when the opportunity arose to tear down some antique hulk and to use the land once more, the new use proposed by the eager redeveloper, as often as not, was inconsistent with the zoning plan. In these circumstances, what zoning board could hold out for very long against the pressure and importuning of the redeveloper? What, after all, was the board proposing instead—more decay, more delay? Was it against progress? Surely, some accommodation, some flexibility was possible.

Even when the land was not already encumbered by structures, many features of the older cities already were fixed, substantially influencing how the rest would develop. For one thing, the ossified street grid itself was in place, fixing some of the dimensions of homes and industrial sites. For another, the railroad yards, the stockyards, the power plants, and the garbage dumps had established the general character of many half-occupied outlying neighborhoods. Then, too, there were the policies of the financial institutions which were expected to provide the mortgage money for any proposed new structures. One could hardly expect them to finance a $20,000 home in a $10,000 neighborhood; to underwrite the long-term collection of little parcels over a lengthy period of time; to gamble on the possibility that the city fathers might close an old street or open a new one in order to make some venture possible. For large areas of the city, the die was cast; the city was bound to be more of what it already was.

To the extent that land-use planning has much effect, therefore, it has been in open unencumbered territory where, for one reason or another, a determined and united citizenry has sought to impose some clear pattern of use upon the land. The most conspicuous kind of case in which the requisite openness and the requisite determination came together was in the exclusive suburban communities of the very rich.

You will recall my having observed that the growth of the urban areas had an unkindly effect upon the well-to-do. Their suburban communities had been invaded, their sense of exclusiveness and privacy destroyed by the irrepressible spread of middle-income subdivisions. By the 1920's, however, some exclusive communities were beginning to discover that they had the legal means for fighting back; zoning ordinances, vigorously and scrupulously applied, could arrest or divert the flow. Here and there, one began to encounter such ordinances—prohibitions against structures of less than such-and-such value, prohibitions against lots of less than such-and-such size. Applied in timely fashion, these restrictions managed to preserve the sparse and splendid land-use pattern of a number of outstanding suburban communities.

Later on, following the lead of the pacesetters, various middle-income communities in the suburbs began to play at the same game. In their case, however, the strategy of land use had to be a little different. Unlike the well-to-do, the middle-income group had no desire to exclude members from their communities who might be able to share the mounting tax burdens. Accordingly, they were prepared to admit some industrial plants in their midst, on the assumption that these could help finance the new schools and streets of the growing area. True, the plants could only be those of a certain type—quiet, well-mannered, giving off the aura of a college campus rather than an industrial nexus. But if they met the specifications, they were more than welcome.

Where the middle-income communities could exercise greatest freedom of action, however, was in seeing to it that the poor would be excluded from their precincts. Shacktowns, of course, were already barred; the health and fire ordinances of most towns were sufficient to deal with these. But then there was always the risk that some enterprising builder might divide a site into handkerchief-sized lots, install the basic sanitary facilities, use concrete slabs or other utilitarian materials as his medium of construction, and provide the unaesthetic minimum of decent housing for the upper stratum of the poor. This was a possibility obviously to be avoided, not only for social reasons, but for fiscal reasons as well. Accordingly, the zoning laws and building ordinances were quickly developed to block off the possibility.

Most communities, too, whether middle- or upper-income in their style, have gradually become aware of another clear and present danger—the danger that the older and more commodious structures in their midst, too obsolete to be used much longer by the income group for which they were first designed, may be divided and subdivided into spaces for the poor. At this stage in a community's development, the monolithic façade of community interest is cracked, broken by the internal conflict between the holders of the new homes and the sellers of the old. This development will not easily be prevented, therefore. Here and there, communities will be invaded by the poor.

Once more, the rich will be pushed outward, even further from their jobs and interests in the central city. Once more, the middle-income group will move on, placidly pulling their job market with them. Once more, the poor will spread out, in the expanded leavings of their financial betters.

There are three or four aspects of the pattern which need concern us, whether we are poor or rich, city-oriented or otherwise. The first point to be made, of course, is that land-use planning in any comprehensive sense really does not exist in our larger urban areas. What does exist is a complex game of chess among localities, each attempting to palm off the undesired applicants for space upon their neighboring communities. This is warfare, not planning. Those who are "for" local planning in any community are dubbed altruistic and "good"; those against are "bad." The purposes of those who are against planning may be no less self-centered than the purposes of those who are for; but neither position must be confused with altruism or with the interests of the urban area as a whole.

The kind of land-use planning that is needed for the major urban areas of America is planning which takes cognizance of the total land-use needs of the area. The localities will have to turn in their weapons of war to some authority whose mandate is broader than their own and will have to be prepared to accept the decisions which issue from that higher level. The authority may be made up of local representatives; it may be something less than a court of last resort. But until such an authority exists in some effective form, we shall have to accept the fact that the planning which exists in our urban areas is incapable of doing much to improve the area as an economic or social unit.

We seem so far from having achieved the necessary organization for effective urban planning that it may appear gratuitous to speak about the policies and techniques of a group charged with that objective. So I shall confine myself to no more than a few footnotes on the subject. One of the first objectives of a group of this kind must be that of defining and preserving the land areas which will be needed for public use in time to prevent their being completely pre-empted by private uses. This should not be confused with a plea on my part for more parks and more green belts. I have little knowledge and few convictions on the question of whether the public needs or would use more open space for recreation. It is a much more simple point that I am making. Although each locality concerns itself with land for its immediate public purposes, no level of government really worries about the preservation of land for more general public use, whatever that use may be. The localities usually try to push common land-use needs off their shoulders onto the shoulders of others. "Everyone wants the water, but no one wants the reservoir," to quote a waggish phrase which is particularly apt. . . . And although the localities are too close to the problem, the state government is usually too far away. Few states can be made to concern themselves very much with the detailed land-use needs of their urban areas. So we are back to a familiar problem in government structure, that of creating a body of authority which is bigger than a breadbox but smaller than an elephant—more extensive in its scope than the localities but less extensive than the state.

One more point of general applicability. Events of the past few decades, as I read them, are proving that the zoning powers which are usually reserved to the city or to the suburban community are simply not enough to insure the use or reuse of land according to any given land-use pattern on which general agreement had previously been reached. The pressures upon a zoning board applied by a private investor who is ready and eager to move ahead on some plan of redevelopment are so great as almost to be irresistible.

This is a problem, of course, which everyone concerned with land-use planning appreciates very well. As a consequence, an old concept is being brushed off and re-examined with considerable interest for its possible application to the current planning problem. This is the notion that the authorities which are responsible for planning the use of land should have the power not only to zone land but also to buy various kinds of property rights short of outright ownership. This property right could be an easement for limited public purposes; it could be a development right which excluded certain private uses from the land; or any one of half a dozen other forms of interest. In any case, the sacred institution of property—one of the most powerful of symbols among the *lares* and *penates* of our current civilization—could be turned to the end of insuring the effective use of a potentially scarce resource: the land.

Those who have been concerned with transforming our urban areas have not confined their efforts to the use of such feeble tools as zoning and land-use planning. There have been bolder and more spectacular efforts—the rebuilding of downtown New Haven, the rebirth of Pittsburgh's Golden Triangle, the execution of New York's Lincoln Center, and so on. These great schemes of bold and aggressive doers have added hope and cheer to those of us who cherish the vitality of the cities.

In surveying these works, however, there are two debts we must discharge. We have an obligation to the men who conceived and executed these latter-day Herculean labors to express our admiration for their efforts. At the same time, we owe it to ourselves to appraise these results in cold and dispassionate terms, to determine how relevant they may be to the total problem of urban renewal.

To gain this perspective, the best vantage point is a helicopter. Hover motionless over America's major cities and you will shortly be impressed by two facts: As a rule, only minute portions of the older

areas of our cities have so far been subjected to rebuilding and renewal in the twentieth century. In New York City, for instance—a
city whose activities in this field have been more extensive than
those of any other in the nation—all the publicly supported renewal
projects undertaken over the past quarter century do not cover as
much as three square miles of city surface. Second, the areas of the
city which have been the subject of the most intensive renewal activity tend generally to be in or very near the city's central business
district. Beyond the comparatively tiny compact central business
districts of our giant urban areas, the gray, monotonous jumble of
obsolete structures extends almost uninterruptedly in all directions.

The tiny land coverage of the publicly supported urban renewal
programs certainly does not result from a lack of crying need. By
almost anyone's aesthetic or structural standards, literally hundreds
of square miles in the urban areas of America should long ago have
been torn down. Yet there have been periods of time when uncom-
mitted federal funds have gone begging for lack of acceptable
projects.

Why should acceptable projects have been so hard to find? There
are a number of answers to the question. First of all, one has to
understand that an urban renewal project is usually a partnership
between governmental and private interests; the government pro-
cures the site, using its powers of condemnation as necessary, and
turns the site over to private redevelopers at a substantial discount
from the acquisition price. The private redeveloper, therefore, must
see a possibility for profit; he must see an opportunity to rebuild on
the site and to find renters or buyers for the new properties.

At this point, our harassed redeveloper is between the devil and
the deep blue sea. Shall he plan to build a little patch of new construction—a small oasis in a sea of decaying structures? If so, although his costs and commitments may be small, his chances of
finding renters for his redeveloped properties will be small as well.
For who among those capable of paying the $40 to $50 per room
for rent would want to wade through the filth and insecurity of
the rundown, obsolete neighborhood in order to reach his concrete-
and-brick oasis in the city?

Alternatively, then, should our redeveloper cut a wide swath through the city, with a giant redevelopment covering half a square mile or so? But the alternative is just as unprepossessing as the first. It demands the closing of streets, the rerouting of traffic, the reorganization of utilities. It entails staggering financial commitments. And it requires a judgment of market demand for a supply of housing so large as to frighten off the hardiest developer and the most intrepid financier. In a word, the problem seems utterly impossible. Almost impossible, anyway. For there is one place in the built-up portions of the old cities where, with energy and imagination, there is just a chance that a good-sized project may be carried off. That place is in or near the central business district.

The reasons for which the central business district should be attractive for redevelopment when the rest of the city usually offers so little attraction are all implicit in what I have said earlier. First, the central business district, unlike the rest of the older portions of the obsolescent cities of America, continues to harbor some elements of vitality and growth. The jobs which demand face-to-face communication in America continue to increase as more of our economic activity is concentrated in financial institutions, central offices, law offices, and the like. Not all cities share in this growth, but many do. As a consequence, a number of large central business districts in America promise to register an increase in jobs. Even those that do not show an absolute increase may experience some upgrading in the jobs they harbor. More executives are likely to appear at the center even if the number of clerks, dishwashers, goods handlers, and factory hands declines. This is one of the forces which explains why it is possible for Pittsburgh's Golden Triangle and Philadelphia's Penn Center to rise out of the ashes and find a basis for survival.

The appearance of a larger number of elite jobs at the center, coupled with the growing remoteness of the exclusive communities and golf courses, stimulates the demand for luxury housing close by the central business district. The amounts involved are not very great, measured in terms of the size of the city as a whole. But the demand is nicely concentrated in a tiny area—in or near the central business district, preferably with a pleasant prospect of river or harbor. When all the elements of demand and subsidy are put together, they sometimes provide the basis for tearing down the structures in the thinned-out slums of the ancient city and building imposing new structures on the site.

There may be another major reason, however, why the central business district tends to capture the lion's share of urban redevelopment projects. If one could plumb the minds of the leaders of any large urban community and look upon the urban area as they see it, I am confident of the image that would emerge. Instead of seeing the central business district as an area containing one tenth the city's land and one twentieth its resident population, they would see the central business district as dominating the image. This is the target of the elite's daily commuting trips. It is the area which contains the city hall, the museums, the theater, the night clubs, and the apartments of friends and associates. It is the area in which the history and the tradition of the city are centered. In short, it is the area that contains almost all that matters in the city for most of its civic leadership. No wonder that there should be a strong bias—unintentional though it may be—in favor of the central business district as a redevelopment site.

Of course, even when the proposed redevelopment is in or near the central business district, there are difficulties to be overcome. In the usual case, the structures that must be razed have been used to house the very poor. No matter how far an ancient slum may have passed its peak of crowding, it still can shelter a considerable number of families. By a process which we have already described, the families that remain tend to be the most defenseless of the slum-dwellers—the oldest, the sickest, or the least able. The others, if my analysis is at all right, have already moved on. Some of the stories which emerge in connection with any account of the problems of relocation, therefore, are calculated to wring the heart of the most callous of observers.

Quite apart from the individual misery occasioned by relocation, one may very well raise questions about the wrecking operation from another point of view. Granted the fact that the situation for the poor is improving, not retrogressing, are we yet prepared to say that it is desirable to cut down the supply of housing available to them? Should we not limit the amount of redevelopment to the amount of low-cost public housing that can be built nearby?

These are the questions that public-spirited groups are prone to ask. Reasonable though these questions may appear, they seem to me to lead to a public policy which is misdirected, distorted, and unhelpful.

That the poor need housing, I have no doubt. But their housing needs are growing far faster in the suburbs than in the old cities. It is in the suburbs that one finds the growing job markets for unskilled labor. Unless we are prepared to impose on the low-income groups the added burden of commuting outward every day from the older city sections, we are doing them no favor to rebuild housing for them in the city centers.

True, something is better than nothing. But "nothing" is not the alternative here. The poor, I said earlier, tend to create their own housing supply simply by ostentatiously bidding for it in the older suburbs. I would myself be inclined to speed that process. Instead of building low-priced subsidized housing in the old cities, I would bend every effort to speed the movement of the poor to the older suburbs. Two measures in particular could contribute to that end. First, the money spent on low-cost public housing construction and operation could be used instead as a direct subsidy to assist families in the payment of their rent. Second, the poor of the cities, handicapped by ignorance and fright, could be helped by public agencies in the search for suburban space. This kind of assistance need not be limited to those families which may have been dispossessed by urban renewal projects; in fact, such families are less likely to be outstanding candidates for suburban living space than some of the younger and more aggressive breadwinners who have already shown sufficient energy to pull themselves out of the oldest of the slum areas. Help in locating better space, therefore, ought to be more widely available to people who live in areas of substandard housing.

Indeed, my strong inclination would be to provide public help for the poor not only in their search for better housing but in the whole process of adaptation to the urban environment. The case for such assistance is especially strong in areas where the poor consist principally of newly arrived immigrants. In this setting, a little help can go a long way—help in looking for a job, help in finding living space, help in locating the requisite medical assistance or educational facilities. This is no new idea. But now that we have recognized the utility of easing the adaptation process through the manning of an agricultural field service, a depressed areas bill, and an overseas Peace Corps, perhaps we may be moved to apply the principle more broadly.

Finally, it would be worthwhile to experiment with the relaxation of building codes, in order to make a $6,000 or $8,000 structure a possibility once more. Obviously, one would not want to relax provisions which are genuinely essential to health and safety. On the other hand, it is a little ironic to lock the poor into structures in the old city which are both unhealthful and unsafe in the interests of protecting them from lesser risks in a much more healthful and safe setting.

Urban renewal, however, need not be limited to the type of operation we have just discussed. Some of the land uses of our major American cities, whether or not they were appropriate for the nineteenth and early twentieth century, are ludicrously inappropriate today. The placement of the railroad yards in most cities is a striking case in point. In Chicago, Philadelphia, New York, New Orleans, Washington, Pittsburgh, and many other urban areas, the railroad yards pre-empt some of the choicest and most attractive sites of the metropolis—close inside the urban mass, on river banks. The volume of freight passing through the yards goes down each year. The freight that is left can often be much better handled from new locations at the edge of the urban mass.

One day, perhaps, when present patterns of rail freight haulage have gone to join the dodo bird, the giant sites will be abandoned and may revert to other uses, such as river-front recreation or attractive housing. But before that happens in the ordinary course, if it ever does, railroad managements and regulatory bodies will have to be roused from their lethargy or will have to be overrun by some higher authority. And one way or another, the cities and towns involved will have to be persuaded to relinquish their tenacious grip on a taxpaying property, albeit a dying one, before the property is utterly dead as a revenue producer.

The case of the railroad property illustrates a much more general problem of many of America's older cities. Beyond the immediate limits of the central business district, extending deep in every direction, are many miles of structures which will not be recaptured within our lifetimes. In these areas, in the normal course, we can expect the structures to continue to decay, the populations gradually to decline and thin out, the jobs slowly to fall off in number. The wistful anticipation that young middle-class couples or old childless ones may come flocking back to reclaim these obsolescent neighborhoods is, as I have insisted, quite groundless. Of course, we will always be able to identify some cases out of our personal experiences which fit any pattern we seek. But even though there may be a crack or two in the picture window, it will not be sufficient to spark a large-scale return from the suburbs to the central cities.

I can, however, envisage two contingencies which may set this prophecy on its head. One is the possibility that we may simply run out of urban land in America. If I have analyzed the process of spread correctly, however, this is unlikely to occur for a considerable time to come. The second possibility is that of recapturing and redeveloping urban neighborhoods in vast parcels—by the square mile rather than by the acre. Once a piece of real estate has been acquired which is so large as to insulate it utterly from the moldering neighborhoods around it—once it is sufficiently large to be equipped with its own parks, schools, libraries, stores, and social structure—then the possibility of successfully reusing the land for middle-income living increases considerably.

To be sure, such a pattern of redevelopment conjures up an image of the Golden Ghetto set down in surrounding squalor. But until the social values of America's middle-income groups have undergone a revolution, this may be the only pattern on which the middle-income groups would consider reusing the inlying sites of the decaying cities. And if the middle-income groups balk at reusing these sites, there is no other use of which I am aware that has such extensive land-using needs as to offer a real alternative.

PART IV
Metropolitan Organization and Finance

METROPOLITAN FINANCIAL PROBLEMS

Lyle C. Fitch

Dr. Lyle C. Fitch is First Deputy City Administrator of the City
of New York. He has served as consultant to a number of state and
local governments and has taught at Columbia, Wesleyan, and other
universities. Dr. Fitch is also President of the Institute of Public
Administration, a private, nonprofit research organization that has
devoted a considerable amount of its effort to the study of metropolitan problems. In this article, Dr. Fitch discusses the vital problem of finance.

Abstract: Exuberant urbanism, advancing technology, and rising incomes and living standards, all are expanding demands for urban government services, some of which can be most efficiently supplied or financed
by metropolitan jurisdictions. Since metropolitan areas are the focal points
of income and wealth, the financial problem stems largely from the lack
of machinery. Many of the most pressing metropolitan needs can be appropriately financed by user charges, but these need to be carefully designed to produce the most desirable over-all economic effects. Both
property and nonproperty taxes should be administered by metropolitan-
wide jurisdictions, leaving submetropolitan governments the power to set
property tax rates for local needs.

Continued urban growth, economic development, and rise of living standards almost certainly will require maintaining, and probably increasing, the share of the national product taken in the form
of urban government services. The evidence of current trends and
existing unmet needs indicates the strength of the pressures for
more and better services.

Lyle C. Fitch, "Metropolitan Financial Problems," The Annals of the American Academy of Political and Social Science: Metropolis in Ferment (Philadelphia, Pennsylvania: November 1957), pp. 66-73.

Expenditures of large cities rose by approximately 75 per cent between 1948 and 1956, and total local government expenditures in the corresponding metropolitan areas doubtless increased considerably more.*

Developed central cities and mushrooming suburbs have faced, and will continue to face, peculiar needs. The central cities have had to meet demands arising from population shifts within their own boundaries—shifts which are economic and social as well as geographic. The larger cities are tending to become concentration points of low-income groups and require disproportionately large outlays for welfare and social development. Many cities are increasingly impressed with the necessity for large-scale physical rehabilitation and redevelopment if they are to compete with the suburbs as places to live and do business, and if they are to avoid untimely obsolescence of private and public investment in their central areas. In the suburbs, rapid expansion requires enormous amounts of new capital facilities in the form of streets, schools, recreational facilities, and the like.

The advent of the metropolitan age and the concomitant development of modern urban culture are creating new demands for many government services and increasing standards of other services. Many of the emergent needs can be supplied only by new governmental agencies designed to operate on a metropolitan scale.

This is the root of the metropolitan financial problem: how to divert a larger share of resources to government use, or, more simply, how to get more funds than existing revenue systems will produce, without unduly impinging on private production. (The last qualifying clause is added because one main objective of urban government should be to increase productivity of private firms by providing them with better-educated and healthier workers, better transportation facilities, and so on.) Solutions, even partial solutions, require better fiscal machinery and broader fiscal powers, as well as organizational innovations, at the local government level. Above all, they require public education and political leadership. Most of these requirements are outside the scope of this paper.

* Reference is to the forty-one cities with populations exceeding 250,000 in 1950.

Other articles [have considered] the task of organization of the metropolitan community for effective action; this discussion is concerned with equipping it with improved fiscal tools.

DEFICIENCIES OF METROPOLITAN FISCAL MACHINERY

Metropolitan financial problems arise primarily from the lack of adequate machinery rather than from any lack of capacity. Presumptively, today's large urban communities, being typically the focal points of wealth and income, have the resources to meet their urban needs.

The following deficiencies in the fiscal machinery characteristic of metropolitan areas seem to the writer to be the most important and the ones whose rectification will have greatest importance for the future.

1. Existing revenue-producing machinery is generally inadequate for the task of financing local government functions; this is true of functions appropriate for the conventional (submetropolitan) local government and functions which can best be handled by metropolitan jurisdictions.

2. The extension of activities across jurisdictional boundary lines makes it more and more difficult to relate benefits and taxes at the local government level. In the modern metropolitan community, a family may reside in one jurisdiction, earn its living in one or more others, send the children to school in another, and shop and seek recreation in still others. But to a considerable extent, the American local financial system still reflects the presumption that these various activities are concentrated in one governmental jurisdiction.

3. In many areas there are great discrepancies in the capacities of local government jurisdictions to provide needed governmental services. At one extreme are the communities which have not sufficient taxable capacity for essential services. The most common case is the bedroom community of low- and middle-income workers which has little industry or commerce. At the other extreme are the wealthy tax colonies, zoned to keep out low-income residents.[1]

Three main types of decisions must be made in setting up and financing functions on an areawide scale. They concern:

The services and benefits which should be provided on an areawide basis.

The question of whether services should be financed by taxes or charges.

The type and rate of tax or charge which should be imposed.

Some services and benefits, like health protection and air pollution control, can be provided efficiently only if they extend over a wide area and their administration is integrated; some, like hospitals and tax administration, are more economical if handled on a large scale;* and some, like intrametropolitan transportation, can be controlled satisfactorily only by a central authority with powers to establish areawide standards and policies and to resolve intra-area conflicts.

TAXES AND CHARGES

This discussion distinguishes mainly between general taxes bearing no direct relation to benefits of expenditures, like sales and income taxes, and charges, or public prices, which vary directly with the amount of the service provided, like bridge tolls, subway fares, and metered charges for water.

General taxes and public prices are at the opposite ends of the revenue spectrum. In between are benefit taxes, which are imposed on beneficiaries of a related service, with the proceeds being devoted largely or entirely to financing the service. Gasoline taxes used for financing highways are a familiar example; the real estate tax is at least in part a benefit tax where it pays for services which benefit the taxed properties.

---

* Results of two recent, as yet unpublished, studies indicate that the unit costs of government services may be less affected by the scale of operations than has been popularly supposed. Harvey Brazer's study (sponsored by the National Bureau of Economic Research) of general government expenditures in larger cities, the group exceeding 25,000 in 1950, finds little correlation between per capita costs of local government functions and city size. Werner Hirsch's study of municipal expenditures in St. Louis County, for the St. Louis Metropolitan Survey, shows similar results for some 80 municipalities, most of them under 25,000 population.

LOCAL TAXES

Local governments, within the generally narrow confines of state-imposed restrictions, have shown considerable ingenuity in tapping pools of potential revenue, however small; few things on land, sea, or in the air, from pleasures and palaces to loaves and fishes, escape taxation somewhere. However, most of the principal local taxes used today are loosely enforced or expensive to administer and dubious in their economic effect. Even the property tax is not exempt from this indictment, although its praises have long been sung and its vices excused on the ground that it is the only tax which can be administered successfully even by the smallest local government. The fact is that it has generally not been successfully administered at all, according to most criteria of equity and efficiency. It is capricious and inequitable even in what it purports to do best.

Part of the typical difficulties of local taxation arise from smallness, both in size of jurisdiction and scale of administrative organization. These, of course, may be obviated by metropolitan areawide administration. Efficient collection of most types of revenues requires an organization large enough to afford trained personnel, costly equipment, and professional direction and research. Geographically, the taxing area must be large enough and isolated enough to discourage avoidance of taxes by persons who move their residences or business establishments over bundary lines or who go outside the jurisdiction to shop. When imposed by several neighboring local governments, many taxes involve issues of intergovernmental jurisdiction and allocation of tax bases.

Where taxes are imposed on an areawide basis, one issue of metropolitan area finance—allocation of government service costs among communities—is resolved; allocation is a function of the type of tax imposed. Areawide taxes also eliminate tax competition within the area; however this may not be an unmitigated blessing if competition by offering better services also is eliminated.

To date, the principal revenue sources of areawide public agencies have been property taxes and user charges, although some metropolitan counties in New York and California, for instance, impose sales taxes and occasionally other nonproperty taxes. The problems of granting taxing powers to metropolitan jurisdictions which extend over several counties remain largely unexplored. A bill introduced in the 1957 session of the California legislature to establish a multicounty San Francisco Bay area rapid transit district went further in this direction than most legislative proposals by giving the proposed district power to impose both a property and a sales tax. The sales tax authority was eliminated in the version of the bill finally adopted.*

The difficulties of working out harmonious tax arrangements between metropolitan jurisdictions and state and already existing local governments have been great enough when only one state was involved to block all but the feeblest beginnings beyond the one-county level. They have thus far been considered insuperable where interstate arrangements are involved. For some time to come, interstate functions probably will be financed by user charges, supplemented where necessary by contributions from the state or local governments involved.

In the almost perfect metropolitan area, we would expect to see metropolitan real estate taxes assessed by an areawide agency,** with metropolitan levies for such metropolitan services as were deemed to be of particular benefit to property and additional local levies for local government activities. Only metropolitan jurisdictions would be authorized to impose nonproperty taxes. In general, the permissible nonproperty taxes would include general sales and amusements taxes and a levy on personal income. Business firms might be taxed, if at all, by some simple form of value-added tax.

The following are among the taxes not used at the local level in the almost perfect metropolitan area: gross receipts taxes and taxes on utility services, because of their excessively deleterious economic effect; and corporate income taxes and such selective excises as gaso-

---

* Tax revenues of the proposed district would be used mainly for service of debt incurred in building a rapid transit system and to meet expenses of the district board.

** Personal property, with the possible exception of depreciable business assets, would not be taxed in the almost perfect metropolitan area.

line, alcoholic beverages, and tobacco taxes, because they can be much better administered at the state level.

Along with several others, the revenue sources mentioned above are now being used by municipalities with two exceptions: The value-added tax and the general income tax. The so-called municipal income taxes now imposed in Pennsylvania, Ohio, and a few other states rest largely on wages and salaries. Considerations of equity manifestly require a broader tax base, and the need for administrative simplicity suggests a supplemental rate on an existing base where this is practicable.[2]

The Real Estate Tax

The principal justification for the real estate tax, aside from tradition, convenience, and expediency, is that by financing beneficial services, it benefits property. Another logical function, which it performs very inadequately, is to capture at least part of the unearned increments to land values accruing by reason of urban developments. Special assessments have been widely used to recoup at least part of land values accruing from public improvements,† but no means has been devised, at least at the local level, of recapturing land values not attributable to specific public improvements.

The enormous increases of land values which typically occur as land is converted from rural to urban use and from less to more intensive urban use constitute a pool of resources which can be appropriately utilized to meet the social costs of urban development, if taxes can be devised to tap the pool. Such land value increases, however, seem characteristically to be concentrated in the expanding sections, mostly the suburbs. Available evidence suggests that land values in many core cities have lagged far behind general price levels and in some cities have not even regained levels reached in the 1920's.* In such cases, urban redevelopment, unlike the initial

† As alternative to the special assessment device, developers in many instances are required to provide for streets, sewers, water mains, and similar improvements which otherwise would be provided by public funds.
* Such tendencies, however, do not necessarily reflect an absolute economic declining of the core.

urban development, cannot count on pools of expanding land values; on the contrary land costs often must be written down at government expense if redevelopment is to be economically feasible.*

Clearly the real estate tax must be adapted to the dynamic characteristics of the urban economy. The tax in its present form gives equal weight to the incremental values resulting from urban development, the values of land already developed, and the values of improvements. Several possible new features should be explored. Some of them are: a local capital gains tax on land value increments, special levies on property values accruing after the announcement of public improvements which benefit the whole community, and a differential tax on land values. Of these three possibilities, the last seems most promising, if only because the basic concept is familiar; it has been used in Australia, Canada, and elsewhere abroad, but by only a few cities in the United States.

THE ROLE OF USER CHARGES

There is a case for charging for a service instead of financing it by general taxation if the following conditions are met:

1. The charge must be administratively feasible. Among the other requirements, the service must be divisible into units whose use by the beneficiary can be measured, like kilowatts, gallons of water, trips across a bridge, or miles traveled on a turnpike.

2. The immediate benefits of the service should go mainly to the person paying for it. This condition, not always easy to apply, means that if a person refrains from using the service because of the charge, the rest of the community suffers relatively little loss. For example, the community is ordinarily not much damaged if a person uses less electricity or makes fewer long-distance telephone calls. In some cases, an additional use by a few individuals may greatly inconvenience many others; for example, a few additional vehicles on a roadway may produce traffic congestion.

3. The charge should encourage economical use of resources.

---

* In the long run, of course, one test of urban redevelopment programs is whether they increase land and other property values, relative to the value that would otherwise have obtained.

Metered charges, for instance, encourage consumers to conserve water and electricity by turning off faucets and lights.

One of the most important functions of charges is to balance demand and supply in cases where excess demand produces undesirable results. If the number of curb parking spaces is less than the number of would-be parkers, the space will be allocated on a first-come first-served basis, in the absence of any better device, and there is no way of assuring that space will go to those who need it most. In such cases, a charge may be the most efficient way of rationing space. This is frequently attempted by use of parking meters, although nearly always in a crude fashion. Meter systems could be much improved if the elementary principles of charges were better understood.

Conversely, a charge—or the increase of an already existing charge—is not justified if it results in the underutilization or waste of resources. For example, as an immediate result of the increase of the New York subway fare from ten to fifteen cents in 1953, passenger traffic declined at least 120 million rides per year, the bulk of the drop being concentrated in nonrush hours and holidays when subways have excess capacity. Not only did the community lose 120 million rides per year, which could be provided at little additional cost, but traffic congestion increased because former subway riders switched to private passenger cars and taxis, and downtown shopping and amusement centers suffered to an undetermined extent.[3]

The peripatetic propensities of metropolitan man and the fact that he may consume services in several jurisdictions while voting in only one have disjointed local government fiscal structures in several places. First, the separation of workshops and bedrooms may create disparities between taxable capacities and service needs. Second, the separation of political jurisdictions in which individuals are taxed and in which they require services handicaps the budget-making process; it makes more difficult a rational determination of how much of the community's product should take the form of government services. Third, the necessity of providing services to outsiders, particularly commuters, creates pressure for taxation without representation.

122   *Lyle C. Fitch*

Market Forces

These considerations argue for a policy of structuring metropolitan governmental organizations in order to allow as much freedom as possible to the play of market forces in determining the kinds and quantities of government services to be supplied, subject to the general principles previously noted (section on the role of user charges).*

The market system can operate at two levels: that of the individual or firm purchasing services or goods from a government enterprise and that of the group—for example, the smaller governmental jurisdiction—purchasing goods or services from a larger jurisdiction. The second level is exemplified by the city of Lakewood, California, and several other cities which purchase their municipal services from Los Angeles County.**

One of the principal decisions respecting any government service is the quantity to be furnished. The important distinction between ordinary government services and services provided under enterprise principles lies in the nature of the decision-making process. Budgetary decisions affecting regular government services are political decisions, reflecting judgments of legislatures regarding how much of the services are needed by the community and how much the taxpayers are willing to pay. Not infrequently, decisions are referred directly to voters. The amount of service to be provided under enterprise principles is dictated by consumers, by the usual market test of how much individuals or firms in the aggregate will buy at cost-of-production prices.† In other words, the question of how much is decided by following the simple rule that where demand exceeds supply, the service should be expanded, and vice versa.

* We can go this far without agreeing with Calvin Coolidge that legislatures should make it their business to discover natural economic laws and enact them into legislation.

** Another way of relating charges on particular areas to services rendered is the establishment of special service districts within a metropolitan jurisdiction which pay differential taxes for special services.

† The question of price cannot be disposed of by the simple qualification "cost-of-production," but that question need not be considered here.

Price-Market Test

The price-market test of resource allocation greatly simplifies the problem of citizen participation in the governmental process. Where services and goods are bought by individuals, each consumer takes part in the decision-making process by determining how much of the service he will buy.

Where purchases are by groups, decisions as to how much to spend must be political ones; but the issue of citizen participation can be simplified in several ways as compared with the situation where budgetary decisions are made by large political units. If the purchasing group is more homogeneous than the whole community, any decision is more wholly satisfactory to a larger percentage of the members. Even if the small group is no more homogeneous than the large, individuals may participate more effectively in small-group decisions.*

Although user charges and the demand-supply rule can simplify the budgetary problem, they do not divorce public enterprise operations from the political process; political participation in many decisions is essential, including the crucial decisions respecting organizational form, investment policies, and integrating the particular function with other community services. For instance, the quantity of services to be supplied by a basically enterprise type of operation may be extended by public decision and public subsidy beyond the amounts which could be made available at cost-of-production prices.** In some cases, public subsidies may be necessary to avoid waste of an already existing resource. Public prices too often are fixed to achieve narrow objectives, such as meeting debt service on construction bonds, without regard for their over-all economic effect.

Some of the most urgent areawide needs are appropriately financed partly or wholly by charges. They include the services which are frequently provided by private regulated utilities such as gas and electricity, water, and mass transportation and other

* This statement rests on the not uncomplicated assumption that the opportunity of participating in decisions of a smaller group is a positive value.
** Even more basic is the question, not considered here, of whether enterprises in particular instances should be private or public.

tation facilities, port development, waste disposal, many
nal services, and hospital services.[4]

BALANCING COSTS AND TAXABLE CAPACITY

There have been few studies of the over-all relationship of costs
and taxable capacity in metropolitan areas—although endless attention has been lavished on particular functions, notably education—
and the subject still abounds with unsettled questions. Brazer's
analyses indicate that the relative size of the suburban population
is an important determinant of local government expenditures in
large cities, a finding consistent with the hypothesis that cities assume considerable expense in providing services to suburban residents. Both Brazer's and Hirsch's studies indicate, moreover, that
per capita expenditures on some functions—police, for instance—
typically increase with population density; this may in part result
from the tendency of low-income groups to congregate in central
cities. On the other hand, the worst cases of fiscal undernourishment
appear to be in the suburbs.

This article has space only for several generalizations which may
serve to indicate directions for further analysis:

1. Costs of essential services may be "equalized" over a metropolitan area, either by areawide administration and financing, or by
grants to local jurisdictions financed at least in part by areawide
taxes. Experience with state and federal subventions indicates that
the subvention is a clumsy tool. On the other hand, putting services
on an areawide basis may deprive local communities of the privilege
of determining the amount of resources to be allocated to specific
services.

2. In many cases, the remedy for fiscal undernourishment may lie
in areawide planning and zoning; fiscal measures as such may strike
only at symptoms rather than underlying difficulties.

3. Fiscal stress in the modern American community is often more
psychological than economic. A common case is that of the former
city apartment dweller who buys his own house in the suburbs and
for the first time in his life is confronted with a property tax bill.
It is not strange that he should resist taxes while demanding mu-

nicial services of a level to which he has been accustomed in the city, nor that he should seek outside assistance in meeting his unaccustomed burden.

4. The point has been made that intercommunity variations in the levels of services should allow metropolitan residents to satisfy their preferences as to levels of local government services and taxes and hence promote the general satisfactions of the entire community.[5] Although the argument may be valid within limits, the limits are narrow; they may extend, for instance, to the quality of refuse collection, but not air and water pollution control.

5. Services rendered to individuals in their capacity of workers, shoppers, and other economic functionaries may in some instances be properly treated as a charge upon the business firm involved rather than upon the individual. Suburbanites, like other persons, create real property values wherever they work, shop, or play.[6] This fact refutes the case for a general tax on commuters, although it does not damage the case for user charges where these would improve the allocation of resources. On the other hand, the maintenance of minimal service levels in poor communities and care for the economically stranded, wherever located, are the responsibility of the entire community.

NOTES

1. See Julius Margolis, "Municipal Fiscal Structure in a Metropolitan Region," *Journal of Political Economy*, 55 (June, 1957).
2. See Harold M. Groves, "New Sources of Light on Intergovernmental Fiscal Relations," *National Tax Journal*, 5:3 (September, 1952).
3. For a general discussion see William Vickrey, *Revision of Rapid Transit Fares in the City of New York*, Mayor's Committee on Management Survey, Finance Project Publication, item No. 8, Technical Monograph No. 3 (New York, 1952); Lyle C. Fitch, "Pricing Transportation in a Metropolitan Area," *Proceedings of the National Tax Association* (New York: The Association, 1955).
4. A recent study of metropolitan government in the Sacramento area recommended that the capital and operating costs of water, sewage service, garbage pickup and disposal, and transit "be metered and charged to the new areas receiving them." Public Administration Service, *The Government of Metropolitan Sacramento* (Chicago: Public Administration Service, 1957), p. 144.

   For discussions of transportation pricing see Vickrey and Fitch, *op. cit.*;

also Fitch, "Financing Urban Roadways," in *Highway Financing*, Tax Institute Symposium (Princeton: 1957); and Wilfred Owen, *The Metropolitan Transportation Problem* (Washington, D.C.: Brookings Institution, 1956), Chap. 7.

5. See Charles Tiebout, "The Pure Theory of Local Government Expenditures," *Journal of Political Economy*, 64:5 (October, 1956).

6. Margolis, *op. cit.*: "A priori, there is no reason to believe that the increment in the tax receipts of the central city accompanying the commuter is less than it costs the city to attract and service him."

SOME FISCAL IMPLICATIONS
OF METROPOLITANISM

Harvey E. Brazer

Professor Harvey E. Brazer of the University of Michigan, Ann Arbor, wrote this essay as a background paper for the Third Annual Faculty Seminar on Metropolitan Research held at The Maxwell Graduate School of Citizenship and Public Affairs, Syracuse University. In this paper, Professor Brazer develops fully the final issue raised in our introductory essay: how to meet pressing metropolitan problems in ways that recognize the diverse tastes and needs of metropolitan inhabitants.

This paper is concerned with some of the major problems that arise in connection with our efforts to provide and finance public services for nearly two thirds of the American population which currently lives in areas designated by the Census Bureau as "Standard Metropolitan Statistical Areas." Heterogeneity, in terms of economic function, income levels, social and political preferences, dominant ethnic origins, and so forth, typically characterizes the constituent parts of the metropolitan community, at least in the larger ones. And yet all residents, business units and families, as well as governing bodies, have a common stake in the performance of public services and the levying of taxes in all parts of the area. If a single central problem can be identified, therefore, it must be defined as *the problem of achieving efficiency in meeting common needs and reaching common goals within a framework of action that*

Harvey E. Brazer, "Some Fiscal Implications of Metropolitanism," in Guthrie S. Birkhead, ed., *Metropolitan Issues: Social, Governmental, Fiscal* (Syracuse, New York: Maxwell Graduate School of Citizenship and Public Affairs, February 1962), pp. 61-82. The author acknowledges a heavy debt to his wife, Marjorie C. Brazer, for her many substantive contributions and constructive criticisms.

gives appropriate cognizance to the diversity in tastes and needs that exists.

The general plan of this paper entails our taking up, in turn, the attempt to establish norms or "ideal" arrangements for supplying and financing public services in the metropolitan area, the obstacles in the way of achieving these norms, and the question of how we can most effectively live with or minimize these obstacles.

NORMATIVE GOALS FOR FISCAL ARRANGEMENTS

The establishment of norms of fiscal behavior for government requires that we define the roles we expect it to play. For government in general it is convenient to follow Musgrave's "multiple theory of the public household" which involves, for analytical purposes, separate treatment of public want satisfaction (his "allocation branch"), income redistribution through taxes and transfers (the "distribution branch"), and stabilization of the economy (the "stabilization branch").[1] Where government is expected to assume responsibility for all three, no one role or branch of the budget is, in practice, fully separable from the others; virtually all fiscal actions will have some repercussions of significance for allocation, distribution, and stabilization. And this remains true even if public want satisfaction is regarded as the sole overt objective of government, as, in my view, it must be in the case of local, as opposed to national, government. Nevertheless, we may, in this instance, regard effects on income distribution and stabilization as being incidental and unsought, to be avoided as much as possible. Thus the role assumed for local governments in the metropolitan community is that of providing public goods and services under circumstances in which the national government is presumed to have succeeded in achieving its goals with respect to income distribution and economic stability at high and rising levels of employment with stable prices.

Local neutrality with respect to income distribution is suggested because of the obvious impossibility of achieving any specified goal in this area if thousands of state and local units of government attempt either to offset or to supplement national action. Neutrality with respect to the stabilization function appears to be either desirable or unavoidable for a number of reasons. Local needs tend to be inflexible over short periods of time, being geared largely to changes in the size and character of the population or requiring continuity for their effective satisfaction. Stabilization measures pursued at the local level involve tremendous geographic leakages which give rise, among other things, to serious questions of interregional equity. The lack of monetary powers and existence of stringent debt limits, which frequently fluctuate countercyclically, impose major constraints upon policy. And, finally, mobility of resources in the national economy as a whole may be impaired through local efforts to increase employment by means of public action if such action is pursued at a time when unemployment is high locally but low nationally.

Most specifically relevant to our discussion of fiscal aspects of metropolitanism is the problem of allocating responsibility for public want satisfaction and its financing among the governmental units that operate within the metropolitan community. Our solution hinges primarily on externalities in consumption. At one extreme, if all of the benefits derived from consumption of a good are appropriable by a single individual, so that there are no external economies of consumption or spillover effects, there are no public aspects of consumption involved and neither must we face an allocation problem. But assuming that there are substantial external economies of consumption, and that we are therefore concerned with public want satisfaction, the interjurisdictional allocation problem involves the question of how far from the point of consumption, if one is identifiable, benefits extend. Conceptually, one may distinguish collective goods involving externalities that extend only to neighborhood or municipal boundaries, to county lines, to multicounty regions, to state lines, and finally those that extend to the nation as a whole or even to the community of nations.

The spelling out of a general rule that will provide the specific answer for each governmental function is obviously extremely difficult, if not impossible. However, we can obtain some guidelines for action within metropolitan areas with respect, at least, to some functions. Thus air and stream pollution control obviously involve important externalities that demand their being undertaken on an areawide basis, without regard to municipal boundary lines; the same may be said of arterial urban highways, mass transit, and water supply, with economies of scale adding weight to the argument for multiunit action. Not quite so clear is the position of recreational facilities, public libraries, museums, and police protection. In each of these cases benefits cannot be confined to the boundaries of individual municipal jurisdictions; nor, on the other hand, are they uniformly distributed within the metropolitan area. Complicating the problem is the fact that a function such as police protection encompasses many subfunctions, some of which are purely local, with no spillovers to neighboring communities, while others either involve substantial spillovers or indivisibilities and major economies of scale.*

The question of whether a given collective good should be provided by the submetropolitan jurisdiction or by some agency with broader geographical powers is further complicated by the fact that the issues involved cannot be regarded as being purely economic. We are necessarily concerned with something more than economic efficiency. The heterogeneity found among municipalities in a metropolitan area involves wide variations in tastes and preferences, the pursuit of which must be accorded a positive value. Thus the solution in terms of efficiency in an engineering sense—that is, the most product at the least cost—is inappropriate by itself. The problem may be fruitfully approached, perhaps, by drawing a distinction between those public services with respect to which taste differentials may be expected to be relatively unimportant, and for which narrowly construed economic efficiency criteria may be allowed to predominate, and those with respect to which purely local preferences will exhibit wide variations, with only minor spillover effects. What is wanted, of course, is a voluntary solution that can be achieved through voting or the political process. A solution that

* The failure of statistical cross-section studies of city expenditures to reveal economies of scale is by no means evidence that they do not exist. Larger cities do not spend less, per capita, for police protection than smaller ones, but this is very likely a consequence of the fact that economies of scale may be offset by the performance of more subfunctions under the "police protection" heading. See my *City Expenditures in the United States* (New York: National Bureau of Economic Research, Inc., 1959), pp. 25-28.

may be called for on grounds of economic efficiency may be rejected if members of local communities place a high value upon their ability to influence policy in the functional area involved. And, contrary to the views of those who are among the more extreme advocates of consolidation in metropolitan areas, there is no prima facie reason for insisting that the "efficient" solution be pursued.

In the attempt to define normative fiscal goals for the metropolitan area, attention must also be directed toward the revenue side of the budget. If redistribution of income through the operation of the local public fisc is to be avoided and an optimal allocation of resources achieved, public service benefits must be paid for by those who enjoy such benefits. The problem is extremely complex, even in a purely general setting, because collective consumption, by its very nature, involves benefits inappropriable by the individual, to which the private-market exclusion principle cannot be applied. A tax system under which liabilities are determined by the individual's preferences for public goods is inoperative, because failure or refusal to reveal one's preferences would reduce tax liability while not denying the opportunity to consume.[2]

Within the setting of metropolitan area finances the problem is even more intricate. Here we are concerned not only with the relationship between the individual and *the* government, but with the additional problems that arise because any one government may be expected to supply services the benefits from which accrue to its own residents *and* to residents of other jurisdictions. Thus even if it were possible for a municipality within the metropolitan area to finance its services by means of appropriate user charges and benefit levies upon its residents, spillover effects and consumption by nonresidents would ordinarily prevent an equation of benefits and charges at the margin. Ideally, benefits must be paid for by those who enjoy them, and all who enjoy public service benefits should participate in the decision-making process through which it is determined which goods and services are to be supplied and the quantities to be offered. Such an ideal solution is ruled out by spillover or neighborhood effects of local public services and nonresident collective consumption within the supplying jurisdiction, even if it were otherwise conceptually attainable. In setting out fiscal goals for metropolitan areas perhaps all that can be suggested is that the repercussions of these considerations should be minimized. This may be achieved through the appropriate allocation of functional responsibilities, coupled with the extension of taxing powers to overlapping jurisdictions and the employment, wherever feasible, of user charges.

OBSTACLES TO THE ACHIEVEMENT OF NORMATIVE GOALS

One of the more sanguine and interesting approaches to the theory of local finance in the metropolitan area is that of Professor Tiebout. In it, "The consumer-voter may be viewed as picking that community which best satisfies his preference pattern for public goods," having been offered a range of choices among jurisdictions, each of which has its "revenue and expenditure patterns more or less set."[3] Thus the problem of getting individuals to reveal their preferences is solved, much as it is in the private-market sector, provided that there are enough communities from which to choose and the other assumptions of Tiebout's model hold. These other assumptions are: full mobility, including the absence of restraints associated with employment opportunities; full knowledge on the part of "consumer-voters"; no intercommunity external economies or diseconomies associated with local public services; some factor limiting the optimum size (the size at which its services can be provided at lowest average cost) of each community, given its set pattern of services; and communities constantly seeking to reach or maintain this optimum size.[4] If we add to this list of assumptions the insistence that residents of each community are not only not concerned with employment opportunities[*] but also refrain from venturing into other communities for shopping, recreation, or any other purpose, except when involved in a change in their places of residence, we may, indeed, have a "conceptual solution" to the problem of determining optimal levels of consumption for a substantial portion of collective goods. And as an exercise in abstraction it

[*] In Tiebout's "model" everyone lives on his dividend checks.

may be a solution, as useful, perhaps, as many of the economist's abstractions.

Unfortunately, however, Tiebout's model cannot be said to be even a rough first approximation of the real world. The most pressing fiscal problems of metropolitanism arise precisely because of the very factors he denies in his assumptions. Even if individuals had full knowledge of differences among communities in revenue and service patterns and were willing to move in response to them and their own tastes, income, zoning, racial and religious discrimination, and other barriers to entry to various communities would restrict their mobility. (A low-income non-Caucasian family does not move from Detroit to Grosse Pointe because it prefers the latter's tax and expenditure pattern!) Families and individuals do extend their activities, in working, shopping, and playing, across community lines, so that there is no clear-cut coincidence between one's place of residence and the place in which services are consumed and taxes paid. Employment opportunities do condition the choice of community of residence, particularly for lower-income families, and for all families commuting costs, like all transport costs, restrict choices. And when the existence of external economies and diseconomies between communities associated with public services (or their nonperformance) is assumed away, we have not only thrown the baby out with the bath water, we have thrown away the bath.

Differences in Community Characteristics

A major source of fiscal difficulty in the metropolitan area arises as a consequence of differences among local communities in the characteristics of their populations. As the Advisory Commission on Intergovernmental Relations noted recently: "Population is tending to be increasingly distributed within metropolitan areas along economic and racial lines. Unless present trends are altered, the central cities may become increasingly the place of residence of new arrivals in the metropolitan areas, of nonwhites, lower-income workers, younger couples, and the elderly." [5] Thus although the total populations of five[6] of the six largest central cities declined between 1950 and 1960, this decline was the product of a reduction in the white population, ranging from 6.7 per cent in New York to 23.5 per cent in Detroit, and an increase in nonwhite population which ranged from 45.3 per cent in Baltimore to 64.4 per cent in Chicago.[7] Looking back over a longer period, 1930 to 1960, we find that for the twelve largest SMSA's combined the white population declined from 94 to 87 per cent of total population. But *all* of this decline took place in the central cities, where the white population declined from 92 to 79 per cent of the total.[8]

The Detroit Area Study's findings on the income experience of whites and nonwhites and residents of the suburbs and the central city, for the period 1951 to 1959, reveal some startling contrasts. Median family income rose from $4,400 to $4,800, by 9 per cent, in the central city (including Highland Park and Hamtramck, which are encircled by Detroit), and from $4,900 to $7,200, or by 47 per cent, in the suburbs. At the same time the median income of white families increased by 33 per cent, for the area as a whole, compared to only 8 per cent for nonwhites.[9] The movement of white, higher-income families to Detroit's suburbs, coupled with their replacement in the central city by low-income newcomers, has increased the median family income differential from 11 per cent in 1951 to 50 per cent in 1959.[10]

For Detroit and, one would expect, for other major central cities as well, developments of the kind described have had substantial fiscal repercussions. They have brought a high concentration to the central city of those who are most vulnerable to unemployment in recession and to loss of employment consequent upon technological change, and who tend to bring heavy demands upon welfare, health, and other public services. At the same time the value of residential property occupied per family declines, thus completing the fiscal squeeze.

None of this is new. It has been going on as long as newcomers of lower income and social or cultural values different from those predominating have concentrated in the central cities of our metropolitan communities. A growing difference between present and past experience arises, however, from the dispersion of industry to suburban locations. No longer is the core of the area necessarily the residential location that minimizes the costs of going to and from the job. Thus, strong pressures have developed which have resulted in the growth in suburban communities of conditions once confined to low-income central city residential sections. In some of these, fiscal problems that exist are even more intense than those experienced by the central city because the suburban community which houses the low-income worker is frequently not the location of the industrial plant employing him. Lower-income families no longer necessarily occupy with increasing density the older residential sections of the central city. They are found concentrated as well in development tracts in suburban communities where the tax base represented by their houses is far too low to permit the financing of an acceptable level of public services.*

On the other hand, the suburb may constitute either an industrial enclave, with a very large tax base and few people, or a tightly restricted area of high-value houses. In neither of these cases do fiscal problems of major magnitude arise.

The resulting contrasts in the size of tax bases relative to population may be dramatically illustrated with data from the Cleveland metropolitan area within Cuyahoga County. The range of assessed valuation per capita for 1956 extends from $122,237 in the Village of Cuyahoga Heights, an industrial enclave of less than three square miles with a population of 785, to $837 in the one half square mile area that remains of Riveredge Township. Among the larger communities the assessed value per capita ranges from $1,858 in Garfield Heights to $4,256 in Shaker Heights, with the City of Cleveland at $2,852.[11]

Similarly sharp contrasts, emphasizing the diversity among municipalities in structure rather than size of tax bases, may be seen in the Detroit area. In 1958 the assessed value of residential property in thirty-four cities, villages, and townships comprised 42 per cent of total assessed valuations in these communities. For the City of Detroit the ratio was 40 per cent, whereas for such industrial enclaves as River Rouge, Trenton, Hamtramck, Highland Park, and

* In the Detroit Area the proportions of families with money incomes in 1958 of less than $3,000 were 21 per cent for the central city, 15 per cent for low-income residential cities, 7 per cent for high-income residential cities, 8 per cent for balanced cities, and 11 per cent for industrial cities. See Table 1 for definitions of types of cities. Data from 1958-59 Detroit Area Study.

Warren, it was less than 20 per cent, while at the other end of the spectrum, in the Grosse Pointe communities, and Dearborn Township, the ratio was 85 per cent or higher.[12]

Such extreme inequalities as those in the distribution within metropolitan areas of socioeconomic groups of population and the property tax base give rise to wide differences in expenditures and tax rates. Tax rates and per capita expenditures both tend to be highest in central cities, but ranks with respect to tax rates and expenditures diverge for communities outside the central city. Margolis found that industrial enclaves spend most while levying the lowest tax rates; "balanced" cities rank next on both counts, followed by "dormitory" cities. However, the omission from his data of school district taxes and expenditures results in a rather incomplete and, in substantial degree, misleading picture. It permits, among other things, the conclusion that balanced cities, relative to dormitory cities, fail "to derive fiscal advantage from their commercial and industrial properties."[13] This conclusion is not supported by data drawn from the Detroit area. Here we find (Table 1) that combined tax rates, including municipal, school, and county levies, are about the same for the central city and the residential cities, lower for the balanced cities, and, again, lowest for the industrial cities. The evidence suggests that residential or dormitory suburbs spend comparatively little for municipal functions, but bear a relatively heavy burden in school expenditures and taxes.

Thus, the Detroit Area data support the conclusion that addition to a community of industrial and commercial property does tend to reduce effective tax rates. But broad generalizations can easily be misleading. New industry entering a community may or may not relieve fiscal pressures. The answer in specific circumstances must depend on such things as the capital-labor ratio involved in production, the level of wage rates paid, the demand for the output of the community's economy that emanates from the plant's operation, the extent to which the labor force lives in or outside of the community in which the plant is located, and so on.

Data presented in Table 2 indicate that there are substantial differences between the central city and the rest of the metropolitan area in the amounts spent per capita in total and for the separate major functions. Part of such differences stems from the fact that the area outside the central city is less fully urbanized, but a large part is undoubtedly attributable to the differences in demographic and other characteristics outlined above. Highway expenditures

Table 1

Effective tax rates in the Detroit area, 1958, by type of city

Type of City[1]	Tax Rate[2] (per cent)
Central........................	1.7
Low-income residential............	1.6
High-income residential...........	1.6
Balanced.......................	1.3
Industrial......................	1.0

[1] Detroit is the central city; residential cities are cities in which the assessed value of residential property exceeds 60 per cent of total assessed valuation in 1958; balanced cities are cities for which this ratio lies between 40 and 60 per cent; and industrial cities are those for which it is below 40 per cent.

[2] The effective tax rate is the mean of the ratios of property tax billed, according to local official records, to the owner's estimate of the value of his owner-occupied residential property, based on a total of 515 observations. Validity checks indicate a very close correspondence between owner's estimates and actual market values.

Source: Unpublished data compiled for the Detroit Area Study, 1958-59, Survey Research Center, The University of Michigan.

tend to be inversely associated with population density, so that we should expect them to be higher outside the central city.[14] Rapid population growth requires large capital outlays for new schools, and thus accounts for the higher education expenditures in the suburbs. But with respect to police and fire protection and welfare, the higher population density, lower incomes, and concentration of newcomers and the aged in the central cities all point to the far higher level of per capita expenditure that we find. The last column of the table, which includes expenditures for such functions as health and hospitals, urban renewal, public housing, sanitation, and

Table 2

Estimated per capita direct general expenditures of local governments in central cities and outside of central cities, 12 largest metropolitan areas,[1] 1957

(dollars)

Central City	Total Direct General Expenditure		Education		Highways		Welfare		Police and Fire Protection		All Other	
	Central City	Outside C.C.	Central City	Outside C.C.	Central City	Outside C.C.	Central City	Outside C.C.	Central City	Outside C.C.	Central City	Outside C.C.
New York	257	212[2]	63	106[2]	18	16[2]	28	9[2]	28	19[2]	120	62[2]
Newark	242	212[2]	74	106[2]	7	16[2]	12	9[2]	38	19[2]	111	62[2]
Jersey City	235	212[2]	49	106[2]	7	16[2]	11	9[2]	35	19[2]	133	62[2]
Chicago	200	145[3]	48	82[3]	35	14[3]	8	4[3]	24	10[3]	85	35[3]
Los Angeles	261	202	95	93	16	11	29	26	30	14	91	58
Long Beach	325[4]	202	115	93	25	11	32	26	29	14	124[4]	58
Philadelphia	165	138	49	72	12	23	4	5	23	8	77	30
Detroit	201	200	62	114	16	19	9	3	25	12	89	52
San Francisco	220	230	62	112	11	15	33	23	35	15	79	65
Oakland	232	230	73	112	16	15	30	23	27	15	86	65
Baltimore	199	149	59	71	19	20	18	3	31	10	72	45
Cleveland	183	189	50	85	19	22	12	12	24	15	78	55
Minneapolis	182	194	59	97	16	17	22	15	16	6	69	59
St. Paul	189	194	51	97	19	17	22	15	19	6	78	59
St. Louis	147	125	45	71	10	15	1	3	23	10	68	26
Boston	272	182	48	70	12	17	41	22	37	21	134	52
Pittsburgh	188	132	41	66	13	13	5	3	24	8	105	42

[1] Metropolitan Areas are those defined as of the 1950 Census of Population, rather than Standard Metropolitan Statistical Areas.

[2] Includes Paterson-Clifton-Passaic.

[3] Includes Gary-Hammond-East Chicago.

[4] Excludes payment to the State of California for settlement of oil land litigation, a total of $138 million.

Source: Derived from U.S. Department of Commerce, Bureau of the Census, *Local Government Finances in Standard Metropolitan Areas*, *1957 Census of Governments*, Vol. III, No. 6 (Washington: U.S. Government Printing Office, 1959), Tables 3 and 4; expenditures of counties containing the central city were apportioned according to the ratio of central city to county population, based on 1957 estimates of county population and 1950 to 1960 straight-line interpolation for the central cities; minor amounts of special district expenditures were not apportioned to the central cities.

so forth, presents the most striking evidence of consistently higher expenditures being incurred in the central cities than in the satellite communities of metropolitan areas.

Equity and Efficiency

If there were no limitations upon the mobility of families and individuals between communities, one might contend that neither efficiency nor equity considerations need enter the discussion. If people chose their place of residence freely, it could then be argued that the price paid for living in one community rather than another, in terms of higher taxes paid for a given level of services or a given tax rate paid for a lower level of services, was voluntarily assumed. It might even be reflected in land values in such fashion as to be approximately offsetting in effect. But as long as barriers to mobility exist, through zoning regulations, racial discrimination, and so forth, such offsetting will not occur and neither equity nor efficiency can be achieved.

Equity, in the sense of equal treatment of equals vis-à-vis the local fisc, may not obtain as between equal individuals resident in different communities simply because of differences in the distribution of income and wealth between communities. Thus individual A, resident in wealthy community X, may be expected to enjoy a larger flow of public service benefits at a given tax cost to him than individual B, A's "equal," however defined, a resident of poor community Y.[15] In the absence of barriers to mobility between communities, we should expect B to remain in Y only if wage rates were higher and/or prices, including land values, were lower in Y than in X by amounts sufficient to offset the fiscal disadvantage. If wage rates were not higher or prices lower initially, the movement of people from Y to X should lead to their adjustment in equilibrium at levels that will just compensate for the fiscal disadvantage of living in Y. However, if B, for reason, say, of color, is barred from community X, the adjustment cannot take place.

The analysis is complicated, of course, by recognition of the fact that individuals may live in one community, work in another, and shop in a third. In this case wage rates and prices of goods and services in the place of residence may be unaffected (at the extreme the community may be a "pure" bedroom suburb) and the burden of adjustment would fall entirely on land values, directly or through land rents, and, at least in the short run, on housing values and rents.

Thus far we have ignored the influence on interpersonal equity of differences among communities in the value of commercial and industrial property. If the cost of providing services to such property is equal to its tax contribution, this influence is zero—but such cost-tax equality is extremely unlikely. If industry or commerce brings a net fiscal gain to the community, its residents can enjoy a higher public service to tax-cost ratio than can be enjoyed without it (all other things being equal). Again, with full mobility equity can be achieved, but not otherwise. The same conclusion holds, with opposite signs being attached to relative gains and losses, where the industrial or commercial property entails a net fiscal loss.

Efficiency in the allocation of resources, including those flowing through the public budget, requires a matching of benefits and costs at the margin, from the point of view of the consumer-voter, directly or on his behalf by "best-guessing" political representatives. On the assumption that the principal or only tax employed locally is the more or less uniformly applicable property tax, if the costs of providing public services to nonresidential property are regarded as given, a vote by individuals for a higher tax rate necessarily means that the increase in property tax receipts available for financing services for individuals will exceed the increment in taxes paid by them.* This should bring an excessive allocation of resources to the local public sector, since expenditure benefits will have been underpriced to the individual taxpayer. Inefficiency arises as well from the firm's point of view, because taxes paid under these circumstances exceed the cost of providing services to it.

All this suggests initially that the property tax as we know it

---

* Assuming that they do not bear the property taxes paid by local industry or commerce through higher prices or lower wages, dividends, and rents, and that individuals are concerned with public services only in their capacities as consumers rather than as income earners.

is an inefficient tax instrument. Combined with differences among communities in the metropolitan area in relative size of industrial and commercial tax bases, it produces cost-benefit ratios for business and industry with respect to their inputs in the form of public services that may be expected to vary widely among communities. If individuals as voters act freely and fully in their own self-interest, we should expect the cost per unit of service received by industry to vary directly (if not proportionally) with the local ratio of non-residential to residential property.* To the extent that this expectation is fulfilled, its influence should lead to a spatial distribution of industry and trade that is different from that which we should expect in its absence. Within any region firms will be induced to locate at less economically attractive points than they would otherwise choose, because at more attractive points—where industry and commerce already exist—the cost of public service inputs will have been pushed to levels higher than those obtaining elsewhere.

This reasoning, plausible as it seems, is not consonant with the fact that industrial suburbs appear to levy lower tax rates than other satellite communities. It seems safe to hazard the guess that these lower tax rates are the product of political pressures brought to bear by industry and by the threat that industry will leave, or of efforts to attract new industry, coupled with imperfections in the political process which may be expected to dilute the effective expression of voter self-interest.

The fact that many people live in one community and work in another substantially complicates the decision-making process in the local public sector. It means that individuals live and pay taxes —property taxes and, in some jurisdictions, income taxes—in one municipality while consuming public services in at least two. What does this imply for fiscal policy and efficiency in the allocation of resources to the local public sector in the metropolitan area? Is the jurisdiction in which the individual works "subsidizing" the one in which he lives? This question has generally been asked in the context of central city versus suburb, but it seems equally applicable as between suburbs.

* This neglects the very real prospect that local industry and commerce may succeed in exerting effective political influence.

Since part of their consumption occurs in a jurisdiction other than their place of residence, some consumers of public services are not consumer-voters. This renders the decision-making process with respect to local budgets in the metropolitan area far more difficult to cope with, even in conceptual terms. The usual benefit approach to budget theory requires that the consumer of public goods has either a direct or an indirect voice or vote in decisions as to what kinds and quantities of such goods are to be supplied and financed. But he is not permitted to vote when he is a commuter-consumer, unless the service is financed by means of user-charges, in which case there is no budget problem for either the resident or the commuter. Suppose we consider traffic control on arterial streets providing ingress to and egress from the central business district of the core city. Here, presumably, the commuter-consumer has no choice but to accept what he is offered, and he is offered such services as the resident-consumer voters determine shall be offered. From the point of view of all consumers of the specific service, we are bound to get underallocation of resources to its supply, because the resident-consumer-voter can be expected to be willing to pay only for the quantity and quality he wishes to purchase, the demand emanating from the commuter being ignored.* Alternatively, the commuter may be viewed as reducing, through his consumption, the product available to the resident per dollar's worth of input. This, again, would lead to less resources being allocated to traffic control than would be optimal were the demand of all consumers taken into account.

This line of argument offers one plausible explanation for the frequently stated observation that municipal services are undersupplied, in the sense, for example, that traffic control is inadequate to prevent heavy congestion in the metropolis. The illustration may readily be extended, with similar results, to a variety of other services, including recreation facilities, police protection, and so forth. The problem would not arise if Samuelson were correct in charac-

---

* Unless, of course, it is taken into account by resident individuals, not in their capacities as consumer voters, but in their capacities as income earners who may gain as bankers, realtors, storekeepers, and so forth, through attracting the commuter by offering better public services.

terizing public goods as those the consumption of which by one person "leads to no subtraction from any other individual's consumption of that good. . . ." [16] Unfortunately, however, this characterization applies, if at all, only to a very small proportion of collective or public goods supplied by municipalities.[17]

The central cities of metropolitan areas and industrial suburbs have been shown to spend more per capita, in total and for major municipal functions (exclusive of education), than all local governments outside the central city in the metropolitan area, residential suburbs, and cities located outside the standard metropolitan areas.[18] Moreover, two studies of city expenditures have found that the proportion of the metropolitan area's population that lies outside the central city is closely associated with the per capita expenditures of the central city.[19] Both sets of findings reflect the fact that the number of people for whom the city must provide services is the sum of its resident population and the nonresident or contact population which spends time in the city in the course of the working day, shopping, pursuing recreation, and so forth. Margolis' data on tax rates in the San Francisco-Oakland area add further evidence in support of the suburban-exploitation-of-the-metropolis hypothesis.*

Central cities may, in fact, provide more public services than surrounding communities, but it may be argued that this is a consequence not of differences in tastes, but of differences in needs, some of which are imposed on the central city by the behavior of suburban cities and socioeconomic forces beyond the control of municipal governments. Irrespective of whether or not the commuter "pays his way" through adding to property values in the central city, he cannot be said to share in the high costs of services engendered by the increasing concentration there of lower-income newcomers, including the nonwhite population. The latter, as we suggested earlier, tend to be less educated, more vulnerable to unemployment, and disorganized by moving from one cultural milieu to another that is totally unfamiliar and disruptive of traditional ties and mores. All

* Municipal tax rates range downward from 56 mills for the central city to 17 mills for the industrial enclave. Margolis, "Municipal Fiscal Structure," *op. cit.*, p. 232.

these factors give rise to expenditure demands to which the suburban community is subject, typically, with far less intensity—expenditures in such fields as welfare, police protection, public health,
public housing, and others. To the extent that suburban communities, through zoning regulations and discriminatory practices in
rentals and real estate transactions, contribute directly to the concentration in the central city of socioeconomic groups which impose
heavy demands upon local government services, they are, in fact,
exploiting the central city.

One consequence of the multiplicity of governmental units within
the metropolitan area is that the provision of public services (or
failure to provide them) in one community has neighborhood or
spillover effects associated with it for other communities in the
area. A high quality of police protection in city A, for example,
will be reflected in a lower incidence of crime in neighboring
city B, or efficient sewage treatment by A will benefit its down-
river neighbor B, and so forth. Obviously each jurisdiction will be
both the source and beneficiary or victim of such spillovers. But
even if all jurisdictions "come out even," getting as much as they
give, the existence of these neighborhood effects will have important
repercussions upon efficiency in the allocation of resources to the
local public sector.

In arriving at their decision as to how much to spend for sewage treatment, for example, the resident-voters of a given community cannot be expected to take into account the repercussions
of their decision on a neighboring community. To conclude otherwise is to assume that they are willing to engage in a form of public
philanthropy. Nor can the fact that the first community enjoys
some benefits emanating from the public services of another be expected to influence the voluntary decisions of its residents with
respect to expenditures for collective consumption. The result,
therefore, must be, again, an allocation of resources to collective
consumption that is below the optimum level that would be indicated if all benefits of such consumption were appropriable in the
spending community. At the extreme, public services that all residents of the congeries of jurisdictions want and are willing to pay
for will not be supplied at all, because the proportion of the benefits

appropriable by any one community's residents is so small as to make the expenditure less than worthwhile from their point of view.*

Finally, if we turn the coin of Tiebout's complex of municipalities from which individuals may choose places of residence, we find that business firms are offered a similar set of alternatives in the metropolitan area. And this side of the coin may and does display some very troublesome difficulties stemming from interlocal competition for industry. Efficiency in the allocation of resources requires that the costs of production of industrial firms reflect the costs of supplying them with inputs in the form of public services and the social costs they impose upon the community, such as through pollution of air and water. But if differences in local tax costs can be employed as an effective means of inducing firms to select one jurisdiction rather than another, competition for industry will force local industrial taxes below the level suggested by our criterion. Similarly, if the costs of adequate treatment of the plant's effluents into the air, streams, rivers, and lakes are substantial and can be avoided by location in one part of the metropolitan area rather than another, no one jurisdiction, acting alone, can be expected to be able to enforce adequate control. Thus it is hardly surprising that rivers become open sewers and air pollution occurs.

APPROACHES TO RATIONAL ACTION

The main burden of the foregoing discussion rests on the divisive, constraining, and conflicting interests and forces which emanate from the fact that our larger urban communities are served by aggregations of uncoordinated governmental units. The inefficiencies, in terms of underallocation of resources to the public sector, and the accompanying inequities, go a long way toward providing some understanding, if not explanation, of the major problems confronting metropolitan America. Even if the forces discussed here could be eliminated others would remain. So-called land pollution, for example, may be simply an unavoidable consequence of our unwillingness to restrict private rights in property to the point

* This assumes that some indivisibilities exist, so that supply of the service below a given level is prohibitively expensive per unit produced.

necessary to eliminate it, and there is not in sight a means of reliev-
ing the choking congestion brought by the automobile, short of
prohibiting its use in certain areas or drastically curtailing the freedom of the auto-owner to decide when and where he will drive.
However, achieving a framework in which voter-choice is better
enabled to satisfy the collective consumption wants of urban dwellers will provide a more efficient allocation of resources and reduce
interpersonal inequities.

One approach is governmental consolidation. The further consolidation is carried, the greater is the extent to which spillover effects are reduced to appropriable benefits enjoyed by voter-con-
sumers—that is, externalities are eliminated, as are interpersonal
inequities. This can never be an entirely satisfactory solution, since
border areas always remain. But more important is the fact that
as the area covered by consolidation is extended the greater is the
extent to which divergent interests and tastes are subordinated to
the will of a more distant political majority. Thus efficiency, in
an economic welfare sense, may or may not be improved, and the
further dilution of the individual's ability to influence or participate
directly in political decisions may be viewed as a major cost.

However, no one approach is likely to prove even conceptually
satisfactory, whether or not it is politically feasible. Solutions to
metropolitan area fiscal problems can, at best, only be compro-
mises. The fact is that we cannot achieve desirable goals or objectives in a manner that permits the exercise of full freedom of individual choice. Rather, a modified objective appears necessary, one
that will minimize the loss of consumer sovereignty in the local
public sphere while avoiding a maximum of the inefficiencies and
interpersonal inequities that arise under existing arrangements.

Perhaps a first requisite is the recognition and acceptance by the
states, and to a lesser extent, the federal government, of their fiscal
responsibilities in this area. The states can take several kinds of
action. These might include establishment of minimum standards
of performance with respect to those functions which involve strong
neighborhood effects or which are subject to curtailment through
interlocal competition. Such functions would certainly include areawide planning and air and water pollution control. In the case of

these functions the neighborhood or spillover effects are of such overwhelming importance that their effective pursuit appears to be incompatible with freedom to establish purely local standards of performance and objectives. These appear to be cases which clearly justify the assertion that the primary obligation of people and individual municipal governments "is that of acceptance of some limitation of freedom of action in the interest of the greater good." [20]

A second role that may properly be assumed by the states is the reduction of local differences in fiscal capacity and interlocal competition based on tax inducements to industry and commerce. This objective may be achieved by expansion of state aid, essentially substituting state taxes for locally levied taxes. This approach need not impinge upon budgetary efficiency. If it is well designed, relationships at the margin, particularly in the choice among alternatives in the allocation of resources within the public sector, need not be disturbed.

State assumption of responsibility for certain functions, directly or through grants-in-aid, seems indicated as well, particularly in the fields of welfare, public health, public housing, and urban renewal —functions whose costs impinge with great unevenness among communities in the metropolitan area. Problems in urban transportation, including both mass transit and arterial streets and highways, may be met by the states through a combination of devices, including grants-in-aid, establishment of minimum standards of performance, and direct assumption of responsibility. Justification for such action by the states may be found in the fact that functions such as those mentioned must be performed because of socioeconomic forces that have their origin not in any one municipality but in the area, the state, or even the nation as a whole. They are a response to problems given by the social and technological environment in which we live. If that response is a purely local one, some members of society, those living in municipalities in which such problems may be avoided, are permitted to escape what may be regarded as a universal obligation.

Keeping in mind the fact that our primary objective is to achieve freedom of choice for individual consumer-voters while avoiding the costs emanating from uncoordinated local operations, what approaches seem indicated at the local level? If the states act in the manner suggested, some of the most pressing existing difficulties will have been eliminated or substantially reduced. One nonfiscal requirement would appear to be the elimination of barriers to mobility within the metropolitan community. Differences in zoning regulations will persist, and this may even be desirable, but other barriers are not tolerable, from the point of view of moral rectitude, efficiency, or equity. The more immediately fiscal issues involve traditionally local functions with substantial spillover effects or important economies of scale. Proliferation of special-function agencies or districts which are not directly politically responsible has little to commend it, but some form of politically responsible federalism has much appeal. Alternatively, in some instances, the county government, with broadened powers, may be the appropriate instrument.

The function of either of these governmental forms can only be defined within the context of broader objectives sought in the metropolitan community. As was suggested above, economies of scale and spillover effects may be the forces upon which this definition may rest. Thus a federation of municipalities may assume responsibility for planning, water supply, sewage disposal, arterial highways, and mass transit, all of which involve economies of scale as well as spillover effects. Areawide recreation facilities may also be delegated to the federal body, while neighborhood parks and playgrounds remain purely local responsibilities; the federation may provide central police services in specialized fields of police work, while basic police protection remains a local function; the same approach may be taken with respect to fire protection, education, property assessment, and certain other functions. Financing may be accomplished by delegation of taxing powers, contractual arrangements, and, wherever appropriate, user charges.

The problems related to the fact that many people live in one jurisdiction and work in another would be much abated under the kind of programs envisaged here. They would be further reduced through the extension of user-charge financing and the use of nonproperty taxes. Particularly appealing among the latter is the income tax under which, as in the Toledo area, partial credit is provided for income taxes paid to the employee's place of residence.

More intensive employment of user charges and nonproperty taxes, coupled with the suggested expansion of state aid and/or state assumption of responsibility for some functions, should do much to alleviate existing local fiscal pressures. The deficiencies of the property tax, especially when it is levied at effective rates of 2 per cent or higher, are so manifest as to require that alternatives be sought. Very little is actually known about the effects of the property tax on land use in the metropolitan area, but as a tax that imposes substantial penalties upon improvement, rewards decay, and encourages land speculation that may have high social costs, it would appear to be a major contributor to the economic and fiscal ills of urban areas.

The very nature of collective consumption and the problems involved in attempting to achieve an approximation of maximum consumer-voter satisfaction in a local public sector operating within a predominantly free private economy are such as to defy conceptual, let alone actual, solution. But even conceptual models of the operation of the private-market economy are satisfactory only within the framework of first approximation assumptions that take us a long way from the real world—some would say too far away to be very useful. Perhaps the economist still knows too little about either the private or the public sector to permit him to do more than attempt to point up deficiencies relative to some commonly accepted criteria and, further, to indicate the kinds of actions that may minimize such deficiencies. With respect to one increasingly important part of the public sector, the urban complex known as the metropolitan area, a great deal more fruitful speculation and empirical investigation are needed before we can conclude that the economist can provide the needed guideposts to the policy-maker.

NOTES

1. Richard A. Musgrave, *The Theory of Public Finance* (New York: McGraw-Hill Book Company, 1959), Chap. 1.
2. See Musgrave's discussion of the problems involved, *op. cit.*, pp. 81-84, and Paul A. Samuelson, "The Pure Theory of Public Expenditure," *Review of Economics and Statistics*, 36 (November, 1954), pp. 387-89, and "Dia-

grammatic Exposition of a Theory of Public Expenditure," *Review of Economics and Statistics*, 37 (November, 1955), pp. 350-56.

3. Charles M. Tiebout, "A Pure Theory of Local Expenditures," *The Journal of Political Economy*, 54 (October, 1956), p. 418.

4. *Ibid.*, p. 419.

5. *Governmental Structure, Organization, and Planning in Metropolitan Areas, A Report by the Advisory Commission on Intergovernmental Relations* (Washington, D.C.: U.S. Government Printing Office, 1961), p. 7.

6. New York, Chicago, Philadelphia, Detroit, and Baltimore.

7. Advisory Commission on Intergovernmental Relations, *op. cit.*, Table 1, p. 7.

8. Harry Sharp, "Race as a Factor in Metropolitan Growth." A paper presented at the 1961 meetings of the Population Association of America. Table 2. Mimeographed.

9. Harry Sharp, "Family Income in Greater Detroit: 1951-59," Project 870, No. 1681, Detroit Area Study (Ann Arbor: Survey Research Center, The University of Michigan, July, 1960), Table 2. Mimeographed.

10. *Ibid.*, p. 8.

11. Derived from Seymour Sacks, Leo M. Egand, and William F. Hellmuth, Jr., *The Cleveland Metropolitan Area—A Fiscal Profile* (Cleveland: Cleveland Metropolitan Services Commission, 1958), p. vii. Assessed values may be assumed to be "equalized" because the county is the sole assessing jurisdiction.

12. Data were drawn from the records of local assessing officers.

13. See Brazer, *op. cit.*, p. 65, for per capita expenditures, by function and type of city, and Julius Margolis, "Municipal Fiscal Structure in a Metropolitan Region," *The Journal of Political Economy* 55 (June, 1957), p. 232, for per capita municipal expenditures and tax rates in cities within the San Francisco area. Both sources fail to take into account the expenditures and taxes levied by school districts, counties, and other local governments overlying the cities.

14. Brazer, *op. cit.*, pp. 25, 36, 39, 42, and 56.

15. See J. M. Buchanan, "Federalism and Fiscal Equity," *American Economic Review*, 40 (September, 1950), for his statement of equity in terms of fiscal residua.

16. "The Pure Theory of Public Expenditure," *loc. cit.*, p. 387.

17. For a brief development of this point, see Julius Margolis, "A Comment on the Pure Theory of Public Expenditures," *Review of Economics and Statistics*, 37 (November, 1955), pp. 347-48.

18. See Table 2 in the text, and Brazer, *op. cit.*, p. 65. Margolis' data "Municipal Fiscal Structure," *op. cit.*, p. 232) support this finding.

19. Amos H. Hawley, "Metropolitan Government and Municipal Government Expenditures in Central Cities," *Journal of Social Issues*, 7 (1951), pp. 100-108, reprinted, with supplementary tables, in Paul K. Hatt and Albert J. Reiss, Jr. (eds.), *Cities and Society*, rev. ed. (New York: The Free Press of Glencoe, Inc., 1957), and Brazer, *op. cit.*, pp. 54-59.

20. Hugh Pomeroy, "Local Responsibility." An address before the National Conference on Metropolitan Problems, East Lansing, Mich., April 29, 1956. Quoted in Advisory Commission on Intergovernmental Relations, *op. cit.*, p. 21.

THE POLITICAL ECONOMY OF THE FUTURE
Robert C. Wood

Where are we headed in the management of our metropolitan destinies? Can we muddle through or will some radical change have to occur in order to prevent a breakdown? In this final chapter of his book 1400 Governments, *Robert C. Wood, Professor of Political Science at the Massachusetts Institute of Technology, peers into the future of the New York metropolitan area and concludes that "revolution" is unlikely.*

THE SYSTEMS WITHIN THE SECTOR

. . . The most significant fact about the governments of the New York region circa 1960 is not the size of the public budgets, the number of dollars allocated or about to be allocated to one program or another, or the trends in these budgets and allocations. The most significant fact is that two different types of political systems rule the public sector today—the local governments and the regional enterprises.

The inference to be drawn from this finding is that these systems, by the attitudes of the participants, the nature of the political processes, and the rules of the political game, strengthen the economic trends in being. They leave most of the important decisions for regional development to the private marketplace. They work in ways which by and large encourage firms and households to continue "doing what comes naturally."

Robert C. Wood, "The Political Economy of the Future," reprinted by permission of the publishers from Robert C. Wood, with Vladimir V. Almendinger, *1400 Governments: The Political Economy of the New York Metropolitan Region* (Cambridge, Massachusetts: Harvard University Press, Copyright © 1961, by Regional Plan Association, Inc.), pp. 173-199. Dr. Wood's book is one of the nine volumes in the New York Metropolitan Region Study series, published by the Harvard University Press.

To be sure, the two systems arrive at their positions of negative influence by quite separate routes. That system which we have subsumed under the title of "local governments"—the units of general jurisdiction and their satellites, the small special-purpose districts—is ineffective in the aggregate principally because its parts tend to cancel one another out. The system of quasigovernmental agencies, the authorities and public corporations with programs which leap over municipal boundary lines, buttresses the marketplace more as a matter of conscious design. In this instance considerations of institutional survival often tend toward programs which accelerate trends already underway. But the net effect remains the same: public policy rarely seems to be the initiating force in the pattern of population settlement or economic growth.

There is nothing mysterious, of course, about why this vacuum in public policy occurs. For all their frantic bustlings with economic development programs, land-use controls, and building regulations, each local government, even that of New York City, commands only a small portion of the region's territory. As each strives to preserve its own local identity, doctrines of municipal mercantilism become natural lines of action. Indeed they are close to being the only politically palatable policies so long as both a desire for high quality urban services *and* continued independence make up a common municipal credo. Yet, from the point of view of the region, no common policy emerges from the welter of elaborately and individually concocted strategies of manipulation and maneuver. Instead, there is only a number of options from which businessmen and households can choose.

In a different way, but just as understandably, the present development of agencies with more or less regional responsibilities makes public direction of economic growth difficult. In the oligopolistic sphere of the transportation giants, the half-way house of water politics, and in the complex realm of intergovernmental housing activities, the program most likely to succeed is the one that supports —not contradicts—the marketplace. Success seems to smile on the transport agencies that favor the auto, the housing project that reclaims a potentially profitable downtown site, the water resources program which responds to a present need rather than anticipating

—and helping to shape—the future pattern of development. Though these agencies are concerned with questions of over-all regional policy with a vengeance, typically they ride with, rather than oppose, the main currents in the private sector.

It is these characteristics of the political systems that allow us to discount the programs and policies of local governments so heavily. So long as the individual strategies of individual municipalities are condemned to frustration because of the sheer number of their neighbors, so long as prudence dictates that regional institutions abet the economic forces already at work, public programs and public policies are of little consequence. Costs of urban government may continue to rise, but they will not substantially influence the preference patterns of families and locational choices of entrepreneurs. The most stringent policies of land-use control or the most ardent wooing of industries will not in the end determine the broad pattern of settlement. While these systems continue, the economist is safe in basing his projections on a consideration of the economic factors involved in regional growth.

CHECKLIST FOR A REVOLUTION

But will the political systems continue to function in 1970 or 1980 or 1985 as they have today? Is it plausible to expect that the changes in living and working patterns projected elsewhere in this study will take place while political styles remain unaffected? Already, in Dade County, Florida, one metropolitan area in the United States has effected a comprehensive structural reorganization and there are more modest but nonetheless significant reforms in other metropolitan centers. Already, one distinguished scholar of urban affairs speaks of "a vast and growing dissatisfaction with life in and around the great cities" and suggests that popular action is impending.[1] Within the New York region itself in recent years, new governmental agencies have been established, new procedures for intergovernmental collaboration have developed, and new proposals for more fundamental rearrangements have been put forward. With such apparent signals of impending change flying, is it conceivable that twenty-five years will pass without the emergence of a new ideology and structure of public bodies, equipped with new capacities and motivations to intervene in the affairs of the private sector? In short, is not the gravest danger in sketching the region of the future that of underestimating—or even ignoring—the prospects of revolution?

This sort of proposition is a difficult one to tackle—but it is not an impossible one. It is difficult because the question is not how much government but what kind of government, and in this instance the projection of trends "as they are" may confuse rather than clarify the issue. But the proposition remains manageable, for there is nothing inherently unpredictable about the process of radical change. We are not called upon to contemplate a disorderly or violent future for the New York region; we are not involved in the business of forecasting municipal socialism or conjuring up visions of irate citizens marching on City Hall. We are asked instead to consider whether certain major stresses and strains in the public sector will require transformations in political habits and major new governmental arrangements—not marginal changes but changes of the character not seen since the boroughs of New York City formed a more perfect union or the Port of New York Authority was established.

Conceived in these terms, the inquiry becomes both a familiar and a limited one. It is familiar because we are covering ground for the New York region which has been carefully examined elsewhere before in the hundred-odd studies of the conditions requiring governmental reorganization in metropolitan areas which have been authorized since World War II. So the situation in New York has strong parallels to Miami and Toronto, where reorganizations were put into effect, and to St. Louis and Cleveland, where they were rejected.

The inquiry is limited, because three specific stresses are involved in the New York situation. We are concerned first with the capacity of the present systems to remain financially solvent, given the pattern of population movement and economic change projected elsewhere in the New York Metropolitan Region Study. Second, we need to make a judgment about the ability of the systems to improve service levels, at least at a rate approximating that since

World War II, against the background of new public demands and new expectations of government. Finally, we have to evaluate the sporadic displays of public dissatisfaction over the ways the region is developing and judge how serious is the inclination for widespread public intervention.

If we can establish a plausible case that the present systems can handle these problems, then our prognosis will be against a local revolution. For our presumption is that the governments in the New York region will continue doing business as usual unless there is compelling evidence that a breakdown is at hand. Ideological satisfaction, historical lethargy, and the calculus of politics are on the side of the status quo. Prudent politicians, committed to the present systems as "going concerns" and uneasy at the uncertainties of change, will, we expect, make minimal—not maximal—adjustments.

THE BURNING ISSUES: (1) THE CASE FOR MUNICIPAL BANKRUPTCY

By all odds, the most widely publicized basis for expecting dramatic changes in the structure of the region's governments and the reallocation of duties and responsibility is the one built upon the so-called gaslight government thesis. The bare bones of this position are that the revenue base of local government is hopelessly antiquated, narrow, inefficient, and inadequate. Local revenues—so the argument runs—are far less sensitive to changes in income or production than are federal or state taxes. Particularly the property tax fails to expand its yield proportionately with other revenues, and yet the structure of local government is such that other tax sources are even less politically or administratively feasible. As a consequence, the region's governments are rapidly approaching the point where they cannot provide even the additional services required by population growth or the extension of urban settlement. With such a rigid tax base they face fiscal disaster—unless there occurs a major overhaul, at least in the revenue system and more likely in the formal structure of government.

In one sense, this argument is only a regional variation of a na-

tional analysis: a conviction that the region's plight is symptomatic
of nationwide conditions. Otto Eckstein, for example, projecting
net cash expenditures of all state and local governments in the
United States to 1968 on the bases of "past policy decisions and the
interplay of political and economic forces," arrives at a "medium
projection" in current dollars of $53.7 billion, in comparison with
the 1958 total of $36.2 billion. On the assumption that present reve-
nue rates and sources will remain unchanged, he forecasts a state
and local deficit of $3.4 billion by 1968—a ten-year increase of $1.7
billion. Eckstein believes that, if conditions of inflation intensify, the
situation will become even worse, for "property tax assessments
notoriously lag behind value changes; gasoline and other specific
taxes also lag; only income and general sales taxes may have a better
than proportionate response." Even without inflation, an average increase in tax rates of 8 per cent would be required between 1958
and 1963 to erase the deficit.[2]

But, if local governments everywhere are headed for deficit
spending, their prospects for borrowing the money they need also
seem dim. Paralleling Eckstein's estimates of total expenditures and
revenue for the future, Harry L. Severson has projected new construction costs, program by program, for the next decade. He arrives
at a capital outlay total for state and local governments in 1968 of
$25.2 billion, and estimates the new state and local bond offerings of
that year at $16.3.[3] Both of those figures are more than double the
1958 levels. But even as the rate or volume of borrowing increases,
the position of these governments in the security market grows
worse. Fiscal experts attribute this partly to the depressant effect
that expanded offerings would have on the market. Another reason
is that the tax-exemption proviso of local bonds is no longer the
drawing card it once was. "The natural size of the market has been
narrowing while the demand for funds has been broadening. State
and local governments have had to bargain away most of the advantages of tax exemptions to investors. Prospects for an increased
interest rate, greater difficulty in securing investors in the marketing
of general obligation bonds seem to compound the financial troubles
of the local unit. The lone investor with the large income who was
forced to state and local purchases in order to reserve some of his

earnings from the National Treasury no longer is sufficient to handle the volume of offerings now current. The relative bargaining position of borrower and lender has consequently shifted and major reforms seem necessary if this source of finance is to prove adequate to the demands ahead." [4]

At the level of the New York metropolitan region, this national analysis is, by the testimony of many observers, doubled in spades. Not since the 1920's, for example, has New York City been able to receive a clean bill of financial health from any of the numerous state or municipal investigating commissions. Typically, the city is usually characterized as operating in a financial strait jacket, with a tax base that cannot meet even the requirements of normal growth. So, the Temporary Commission on the Fiscal Affairs of the State Government concluded in 1955 that, by 1961, the city would require $511 million more than in the 1954-55 budget and that only about one half of the increase could be received from the existing tax levies.[5] (As it turned out, the predictions came true three years before the 1961 target date.) Continuing the tradition, the Commission on Governmental Operations of the City of New York, established in 1959, observed that between 1949 and 1958 the city's total operating costs increased by almost 82 per cent while the property tax base estimated at market value expanded by only 56 per cent and the residents' personal income after income tax withholdings rose by only 23 per cent.[6]

The city's capital outlay program is similarly in tight circumstances. In 1958 the Planning Commission set the capital requirements for the city at $300 million annually for a "barely minimum capital program." An adequate program over the next ten years, in the commission's judgment, would call for a yearly expenditure of $380 million and even this would only "permit reasonable progress in meeting our real needs without frills. It makes no allowance for increased costs and it would not permit any major additional transit expenses." In contrast, the actual capital expenditure had not exceeded $200 million in any postwar year to 1958 and is not budgeted to go much higher in the years immediately ahead.[7]

The largest city in the region is not the only one that appears, on the surface, to have reached the limits of its revenue yields. Surveying in 1959 the postwar experience of the region's suburban governments, Merrill Folsom reports a growing concern over the present level of taxation among officials and residents; cries of "strangulation" as "the real estate tax burden is being shifted from the urban industrial areas to the new homes of commuters"; and statements that "taxes are becoming overwhelming." Within affluent Westchester County, where real estate levies increased from $61.5 to $136.7 million between 1948 and 1958, Folsom calculated that at current levels, an average property-owner's lifetime taxes on real estate will be $7,710.[8]

Less impressionistically, Samuel F. Thomas supplements Folsom's finding, focusing on the extraordinary growth in school expenditures in Nassau County. Between 1945 and 1954, Thomas reports, school operating expenditures rose over 300 per cent and total school expenditures went up 657 per cent. In the one year between 1953-54 and 1954-55, the school operating expenditures rose by one third, leaving Thomas to suggest "that the tax burden on the real estate owner in Nassau County is greater and is increasing at a faster pace than the tax burden on the property-owner in New York City." [9]

Perhaps the bluntest warning of tax insufficiency in New York has come from New York State's Commissioner of Education, James E. Allen, Jr. Anticipating necessary educational outlays in New York in 1965 at double their 1958 level, Allen estimates that—even having made "liberal allowances for the growth of real property valuation" in the meantime—local property tax rates would have to increase by about 40 per cent to finance new school budgets. In his judgment "the real estate tax will not suffice for meeting the educational burdens of the years immediately ahead." [10]

The same cries of tax crises echo with special intensity in New Jersey. With a much heavier dependence on the property tax, the Garden State has doubled the amount so levied between 1948 and 1958. The New Jersey Commission on State Tax Policy in its 1958 report concludes, "The policy of no new taxes has succeeded only in part. Its success has been limited largely to the legislative halls. Its effect may well have been to commit New Jersey to the support of its governmental services primarily from the property tax to the point of no return." [11]

Paper Tigers in Public Finance

But what precisely is "the point of no return" in estimating the capacity of a tax system? One is not disposed to ignore steadily rising tax rates nor prophecies of disasters when issued by responsible observers. Nonetheless, the minor and often underemphasized premise of the municipal bankruptcy argument is that there is somewhere an economic or political peril point beyond which taxes cannot go without the system collapsing. Specifically there is the notion that Eckstein's 8 per cent increase in effective taxes (that is, tax levels expressed as a percentage of tax base, either income or market property value) is very hard to come by in the world of practical affairs.

Yet, actually, the facts do not bear out this contention. Once expenditure and revenue trends are laid along trends in economic growth, more than a little sunshine breaks through the gloom. On a national basis in 1958, after a decade of dramatic growth in absolute terms, total expenditures of local governments amounted to 5.8 per cent of the gross national product—about the same as in 1927. State and local capital expenditures in the same period closely paralleled earlier experience; they totaled 2.4 per cent of the gross national product in 1955 as contrasted to 2.1 per cent in 1927.[12]

Nor do the years ahead appear to place substantially more drastic burdens on the economy. Eckstein's projections of expenditures assume that state and local expenditures will move in the 1958-68 period from 8.3 per cent of the gross national product to 8.6 per cent—certainly not an extraordinary rise.[13] Making similar forecasts, Dick Netzer arrives at a 1970 "moderate" projection in the range of between 8.4 and 8.9 per cent of the gross national product.[14] His "substantial" projection—the highest range of expenditures which he believes possible—is between 10 and 10.6 per cent. Other analyses project a 1970 state-local ratio of expenditures to gross national product at approximately 10 per cent.[15]

When we move to the most accurate indicators of "available" revenues—real property valuations and tax rates expressed as a percentage of market value—the desperate straits of local fiscal capacity seem even less desperate. Despite the persuasive logical arguments to the contrary, nationwide the property tax has proven far from sluggish in recent years. Netzer estimates that between 1946 and 1957 the percentage change in the property tax base for all state and local governments was about 151 per cent, an increase just about equal to that of the gross national product. During the same period, the increase in the average effective tax rate—as a proportion of value—has been about 5 per cent, and between 1946 and 1952 the effective tax rates across the country appear actually to have declined.[16]

Once again, the evidence which can be assembled on a regional basis supports a conclusion that the experience of the New York metropolitan region parallels that of the nation. As a proportion of personal income, total local government *expenditures* rose between 1945 and 1955 from 5.9 per cent to 9 per cent for the total region, from 5.7 per cent to 10.3 per cent for New York City, from 7.0 to 9.3 per cent for other New York governments and from 5.9 per cent to 6.4 per cent for New Jersey units. No dramatic signs of upheaval in local *revenue* burdens appeared. As Table 1 indicates, total property tax levies show no sharply rising trend relative to personal income outside New York City. Further, our investigations in New York State indicate that total local property taxes as a percentage of market value declined between 1950 and 1955 an average of 30 per cent for the governments in the counties outside New York City. A further indication of the "water" remaining in the existing tax structure is the fact that in 1951 the average ratio of the assessed valuation to market value for the New Jersey counties of the region was 33.1 per cent and in 1957 was 28.7 per cent.[17] Throughout a decade of substantial population changes and pent-up demands for public services spilling over from the war years, New Jersey has maintained its policy of "no new taxes" because it extracted over one half billion dollars in additional revenue from the taxes it already had.

It is true that local school taxes on real property rose considerably, in absolute terms, an average of 121 per cent between 1950 and 1955.[18] But when these school taxes are shown as a percentage of personal income and of market value of property (where these figures were available), the increase is not so sharp. Here the New York experience again approximated that of the nation: local school

Table 1

Total property tax revenue of local governments compared with personal income[1] of population, New York metropolitan region[2]

	Personal income (millions)	Local property taxes (millions)	Property taxes as percentage of income
Region			
1945...............	$20,287	$ 619	3.05
1950...............	27,876	998	3.58
1955...............	35,766	1,495	4.17
New York City			
1945...............	13,124	300	2.28
1950...............	16,247	541	3.32
1955...............	18,663	763	4.08
Other New York counties			
1945...............	2,412	112	4.64
1950...............	4,328	161	3.71
1955...............	6,814	305	4.47
New Jersey counties			
1945...............	4,751	207	4.35
1950...............	7,301	296	4.05
1955...............	10,289	427	4.15

[1] Personal income figures for 1945 and 1950 were interpolated from New York Metropolitan Region Study estimates for 1939, 1947, and 1955.

[2] Excluding Fairfield County, Connecticut, for which figures are not available.

taxes doubled, but in the relatively low range of from 1.5 to 3.0 per cent of personal income.

In summary, these figures suggest that however intense the spending pressures in the region's public sector generated by urbanization and growth since World War II may appear for the region as a whole, they have certainly not brought about a massive diversion of income or capital to public purposes. More important, in an economic sense (except possibly for a long-term shift in consumer expenditures away from housing expenditures and a consequent slowing down in the accumulation of taxable property values) the resilience of public revenue does not seem as low as is often supposed. For the "gaps" between projected expenditures and projected revenues, more often than not in the postwar period, have been filled by an increase in revenue rather than a reduction in expenditures, demonstrating an elasticity in taxes not suspected when the trends of expenditures and revenues are extrapolated independently of one another. In the end, the case for municipal bankruptcy rests on the incapacity of the political process to divert funds to public policy—not on "an objective economic constraint to taxes . . . or a measurable limit on the fraction of economic activity that a community may wish to channel through the public sector." [19]

But this supposed political incapacity has not shown itself in the New York metropolitan region. In New York City, beginning with the complete reorganization of grants-in-aid under the Moore Plan in 1946, continuing in the state's uniform reassessment of local property values, and extending to Governor Rockefeller's proposal to equip the local school districts with general powers of taxation, again and again the size of the revenue structure has been expanded.[20] Less dramatically, New Jersey has moved in the same direction: first, by a grant-in-aid breakthrough so far as education is concerned; second, by the business earnings tax in 1958; third, by the court rulings on assessments which in effect have doubled the taxing capacity of all local jurisdictions. When these state actions are coupled with the adoption of local sales and nuisance taxes at the county and municipal level, and with much heavier rates of borrowing, it is clear that over-all the political process has displayed few signs of incapacity to adjust. Simultaneously, it has indicated little disposition to undergo comprehensive or fundamental structural or financial reform.

It is quite true that this picture of the regional public sector as a whole does not fit equally well all parts of the region. On a relative basis, not only New York City but the older municipalities in the inlying New Jersey counties have experienced conditions of increasing stringency. In the six years between 1951 and 1957, Jersey City, Newark, Elizabeth, Paterson, Bayonne, and Hoboken have all faced increased tax rates against a background of tax bases which were either rising much more slowly or actually declining. These six registered changes of between 2.2 per cent and 45.9 per cent in the local property tax rate per thousand dollars of full market value. In the case of Hoboken and Bayonne, where the increases were 45.9 per cent and 12.2 per cent respectively, these changes were accompanied by absolute losses in both assessed and market value. Clearly, these cities have not found the last few years easy going.

Yet these municipalities still seem more the exception than the rule—there is little evidence that the division between the haves and the have-nots in other parts of the region grows worse. On the contrary, what little evidence can be assembled hints at an opposite process underway. When New York towns were compared in the estimated per capita full market value of taxable property for the years 1945, 1950, and 1955, no trend toward greater disparities among the governments' revenue base was detectable. Although there is an increasing spread in the values of these series (as indicated in the increase in the standard deviation from $1180 in 1945 to $2350 in 1955), the degree of dispersion relative to their average level remains roughly the same.[21]

Very probably even the absolute increase in the ranges of these values reflects more the regionwide growth in property holdings and the impact of inflation than any tendency toward an increasing "clustering" of values. One can reason from this pattern that, though differences in residential values among localities continue to grow, the process of commercial and industrial diffusion works in the opposite direction. New shopping centers and new industrial plants leaven the sprawl of comparatively low-value residential settlement in Bergen, Rockland, and Suffolk Counties to offer tax relief to beleaguered officials.

Clearly we are on tenuous ground either in forecasting that the older cities will muddle through or that the respective positions of the haves and have-nots will stay about the same. For one thing, a ten-year time is too short to determine reliably what is happening to the spread in municipal tax bases. For another . . . municipalities *try* very hard to acquire that kind of residential and industrial development which returns more in taxes than it costs in public services, and intent becomes entangled with effect. Undoubtedly once a government scores an initial success in this strategy a snowballing tendency may get underway—for it is easier for "them that has" not only to "get" but to get more. Still there are few signs, as we have seen, that these intentions are generally matched by deeds. To the contrary, a gradual bunching of effective tax rates is underway, and a leveling out in the per capita differences in respective tax bases. As another volume in this study has pointed out: "The scope for variation in the tax levels of different areas contained within a single state is narrowing. More and more of the total tax bill is coming to be represented by state and federal taxes, correspondingly less of it by local taxes . . . on top of this, the leveling of population densities in the region of the future may well add to the general equalization of local tax rates." [22]

THE BURNING ISSUES: (2) THE DEMAND FOR SERVICES

If one can feel sanguine about the future supply of public monies in the region, what other pressures might drive the governments to radical reform? Paradoxically enough, the very fact that public budgets *can* be balanced is often taken as a distress signal. The second major indictment of the present systems is that expenditures are set now and in the future at far too low a level. Malnutrition, not galloping consumption, according to this argument, is the fatal ailment of the public sector.

This is by no means a new argument in the United States, but it is an especially fashionable one right now. Its main thrust is that the American economy suffers from underspending so far as social investment and services are concerned; that national prosperity depends on channeling more resources to the support of government. Or, in one of the more pungent phrases of its advocates, the present mechanisms for allocating resources between the public and private sectors pay too much attention to "private wants" and not enough to "public needs." [23]

One can catch a sense of what the New Spenders regard as appropriate expenditure levels by reviewing the "needs" established by professional specialists in the main public programs. Writing in 1955, and concerned with projecting government expenditures to 1960, Wilie Kilpatrick and Robert Drury attributed past changes in expenditures to such relatively impersonal and typical forces as prices, population growth, age distribution, income, and urbanization. Looking to the future, however, they distinguished between demands and needs and provided two 1960 estimates: the "probable" and the "needed," according to the lights of experts in the public programs involved. Wherever a "direct measure of need" was available, the authors employed it, usually maintaining the same ratio between probable and needed expenditures for 1960 as existed in 1950. In their calculations, total state and local expenditures in 1960, using 1950 prices, would "probably" total $37 billion, whereas $42 billion would be actually "needed." Thus, a series of "deficiencies"—the gaps between the probable and the needed—appeared: $1 billion for schools, $165 million for highways, $455 million for welfare and corrections, and so on, adding up to a grand total of over $5 billion.[24]

The same sort of balance, this time for public investment rather than annual spending, was struck in 1957 by the Special Assistant to the President for Public Works Planning. His office estimated a backlog of $204 billion worth of public facilities required by 1965, including $92 billion for highways, $42 billion for education, $22 billion for hospitals, and $25 billion for water and sewage. In effect, the Special Assistant called for construction spending at the rate of $20 billion at a time when the annual rate was 42 per cent of that amount.[25]

Yet, just as with the bankruptcy argument, the starvation thesis fails to come to grips with the reality of the problems of the public sector. Estimates of needs can put dollar signs on the expectations of experts concerned about the quality of public service today—but they cannot turn the preferences of the experts into the preferences of the public. Even if they could, the popular preferences would not be immediately registered on the governments involved. At best, what the estimates give us are standards by which to evaluate services. They never free us from the problems of determining whether any given set of standards actually expresses preferences—or whether any set of standards is likely to be realized. Thus, one can readily admit that the impersonal forces of population growth, industrialization, density, and so forth push up the demand for public services, without arriving at the conclusion that failure to meet certain defined standards courts political disaster. One can concede that while schools are crowded there will be articulated demands for additional classrooms—and that while streams are polluted, there will be judicial decisions requiring the installation of more disposal systems—and still not accept the proposition that these voices and decisions will inexorably prevail. No greater mistake can be made than to suppose that the apparently objective and impersonal chronicling of "requirements" is anything more than presumptive evidence that some individuals are unhappy about the present state of affairs.

What is most relevant in estimating the relation of service levels to political stability is not their deviation from utopia but an understanding of the drift of present affairs in terms of the temper of the region's residents. What we need to know are not the opinions of agitators as much as the general record of recent accomplishments. By and large, are public services showing some signs of improving quality that can be determined in any reasonable objective way? Are the most pressing "needs" being fulfilled first? Are the politically active and influential elements in the region's constituencies mollified by the recent trend of events?

On all these counts, on the basis of the evidence which is available, the record of the region suggests that the systems are more likely to survive than go under. So far as the over-all trends are concerned, it seems clear that improvements in the quality of public services are being registered. Between 1945 and 1955, the average per capita operating expenditure for the region in constant 1954 dollars rose from $160.71 to $221.90, an increase of 35.1 per cent.[26]

Undoubtedly some of this increase may have been the result of the growing complications of providing a roughly constant level of services under more difficult circumstances—extra police assignments in the slums of older cities, for instance, or more fire engines for a new suburban development. Some could also be set down to increased factor costs—changes in real wages and fringe benefits without any improvement in the services involved. But even if we take these aspects into account for the region as a whole, there has been, in fact, an increase in services—in more policemen per thousand population in New York City, more hospital beds in Newark, more teachers per thousand pupils in the New York suburbs, more teachers with an A.B. degree in the New Jersey suburbs. Fire rating improved in Long Island towns; the average age of subway cars declined; school property value per pupil across the region almost doubled. Even in those older cities with stable or declining populations, significant changes in major services seem to have occurred. Between 1947 and 1957, the number of firemen in Yonkers, Elizabeth, Newark, and New York City increased 19, 20, 18, and 65 per cent, respectively. The number of policemen rose 32, 27, 17, and 46 per cent. In short, if, as experts in municipal finance have long contended, the citizen gets what he pays for—if service standards are principally a function of money—quality has improved for almost every service in every part of the region. On a per person, constant dollar basis, more money has been put to public purposes at a faster rate than in any other ten-year period in the region's history.[27]

If the region's over-all performance shows up favorably, what about the record for the services which loom most important in the public eye? As far as the largest public program—education—is concerned, absolutely and proportionately more money has gone into this activity than any other. Between 1955-56 and 1959-60, the average school operating expenditure per pupil in New York State has risen from $378 to $491; and during the 1959-60 school year the foundation "minimum" program amount of $356 was exceeded in 95 per cent of major school districts. Indeed, if one were disposed to accept the referenda on school bond issues as a true expression of the public will, the decision would be inescapable in New York that school progress has been too rapid. For the 1958-59 school year, 38 per cent of all bond issues put to a vote failed to carry.[28]

If the quality of municipal services seems at least to be holding steady, and schools improving rapidly, prospects are just as good for improvements in another sensitive area: transportation. At any rate, facilities for the movement of automobile and air traffic are being constructed at a rate and on standards of service which have never been undertaken before. No one could accuse the Port of New York Authority, for example, of lack of imagination and enterprise in its planning and building of the new John F. Kennedy Airport. The designs of the new bridges and expressways similarly display continuing pursuit of engineering excellence. The gross annual operating expenditures of the Port Authority between 1945 and 1955 increased 170 per cent—compared to an increase by the City of New York of about 80 per cent, and an average increase of 120 per cent in nonschool operating expenditures outside New York City. Only the suburban school districts have registered a greater percentage rise on the average, topping the 200 per cent mark in their expenditure increases during the same period.[29]

Of course, . . . both the school districts and the transportation authorities operate in very special circumstances. The districts have developed sophisticated and financially remunerative relations with state authorities, resulting in large and growing grants-in-aid programs. The transportation agencies are supported by user charges which feed on larger and larger volumes of traffic or substantial federal grants. In both instances, public officials responsible for the programs are able to a considerable degree to define "needs" according to their own standards and then proceed to satisfy them. Given these capabilities, it is not surprising that these programs function on a self-starter basis and their records of improving standards of service are the best in the region.

As in the case of the revenue question, then, the problem of public expenditures in the region turns out at rock bottom to be one of political attitudes and behavior. Just as any allocation of resources between the public and the private sectors from 1 to 100 per cent is theoretically possible, so, given public desires which are intense enough, almost any "need" can be fulfilled. In Lyle Fitch's words, "Fiscal stress in the modern American community is often more psychological than economic."[30] All that our expenditure calculations can yield is the knowledge that, in ways more or less related to the type of government involved, public spending has been increasing, and that one is justified again, with some qualifications, in inferring that quality has been upgraded in public programs. Whether the quality is good "enough" and the responsiveness rapid "enough" are issues which no expenditure series or professional criteria of excellence can answer.

POLITICAL PAYOFFS IN THE GOING SYSTEMS

We have been seeking evidence that a substantial change in the nature of public ideology and organization impends in the New York region—one that will alter the trends which economic analysis has identified. The burden of the foregoing two sections has been that the indices customarily employed to gauge the effectiveness of the present system are not really relevant to the issue. The region's governments theoretically can never go bankrupt, and they can never achieve the utopian standards that program specialists advocate.

But even if we took the indices seriously, the recent history of the region would give us little cause for alarm. No "cruel burden" present or impending seems to rest upon the taxpayer, even if the most pessimistic estimates of new levies are accepted. No abnormally low service standards prevail, at least when considered in historical perspective. What has occurred—when one considers criticism of school conditions in New York City or renewal programs in New Jersey— is a sizable redefinition of what we consider "adequate" today, at least in experts' eyes. What obviously exists is a body of opinion which wants more funds allocated to the public sector and more positive public policies toward the use of natural resources in the region, the planning of the transportation network, and the rebuilding of the region's centrally located cities. The question is whether or not that body of opinion will be politically effective enough in the next twenty-five years to accomplish its objectives.

We should be as specific as possible here about what the revolution would constitute now that it seems clear it will not come with Hegelian naturalness. It would involve, first off, a much more rapid diversion of resources to the public sector: at a rate which, say, diverted at least one half of all productivity gains to government rather than private spending. More important, however, it would involve the establishment of a governmental structure which possessed the jurisdiction and the authority to make decisions about alternative forms of regional development, more or less consciously and more or less comprehensively. More specifically, there would be some type of regional organization empowered to set aside land for recreational purposes on the basis of a regional plan and not on the sporadic acquisitions of states, localities, and independent authorities or bequests by private citizens. There would be some type of regional organization empowered to subsidize commuter transportation, if this were in accord with a general plan. And, to be fully satisfactory to the body of opinion which Jesse Burkhead has termed the "view-with-alarm" school of metropolitan affairs, the organization should probably be responsible to a regional electorate and draw revenue from a common revenue pool.

To sketch the skeleton of a government sufficient to redirect the pattern of economic development in the region—even in the minimum terms above—is to indicate at once the rocky road to reform. For, if the dissidents are to be effective, they must attract a sizable number of politically influential supporters; they must gain the acquiescence of the majority of the region's residents; and, finally, they must overcome formidable legal, constitutional, and political obstacles, to make the ground swell of opinion legally applicable. These are difficult tasks. Slow evolution over the next twenty-five years, not decisive action to alter the main lines of development, seems the course of least resistance.

Perhaps the most formidable obstacle to changing either the structure or the philosophy of the region's governments would be the assembling of a coalition of effective political figures. On the basis of the strategies and policies treated earlier in the book, it is hard even to conceive how such a coalition might come about. At the outset, three governors, the mayor of New York City, and the chief office-holders of the seventeen counties surrounding the city would have to be persuaded that their present performance in their offices was unsatisfactory; that their failure was due to severe structural deficiencies in the present organization; and that only the creation of new arrangements would solve the problems they face.

That these officials know they have problems is already clear. Since 1956, the Metropolitan Regional Council has included in its thirty-man body the top elected officials of all the counties and major cities of the region as well as a number of smaller municipalities.[31] As an informed, consultative association, the council has been able both to develop common policies with respect to some matters of law enforcement and traffic control and to initiate major investigations into regional problems. It has been hailed therefore as having a "great potential for becoming an official regional leadership institution." [32]

The potential exists—but so far the evolution of the council into an agency with the capacity to set goals, analyze resources, and recommend development policies has been slow. It remains a confederation, requiring unanimous consent from all its members before taking any important step. For two years, one of its committees held hearings to determine if it should acquire legal status. But the upshot of this self-analysis remains inconclusive, for although the council has ultimately decided that its role should be legitimized, a strong minority is reported as reluctant to see the organization gain official recognition. Some outside groups have suggested that the council take on operating responsibilities. Among these groups were the Citizens' Union, the Metropolitan Committee on Planning, and the Association of Real Estate Syndicators. But the more noteworthy of the council's supporters—the Regional Plan Association of New York, the Citizens Budget Committee, and the State Citizen Council—have carefully refrained from suggesting that it acquire independent financial resources or assume major operating responsibilities.

Meantime, there are few signs that the usual pattern of political behavior is undergoing a metamorphosis. Officials continue to cling to their favorite slogan—"cooperation"—as the panacea for the very real conflicts of interests which exist. The conflicts themselves, however, show few signs of diminishing. A new state study committee has been created to criticize the city's administration and to cast doubt about the capacity of the largest governmental organization in the region to conduct its own affairs. Recent mayors of the city and the recent comptrollers of the state have continued in the tradition of their predecessors to dispute openly the program needs of the city government. The city and the Port Authority continue to announce and activate separate programs for port development. The New Jersey municipalities and the Port Authority continue to disagree on their respective responsibilities with respect to a metropolitan district plan for pooling transit revenues. As between the states themselves, problems over the taxation of New Jersey residents by New York, of air pollution control, and the strain of persistent crises in mass transportation have led to predictions of "an era of hostile rivalry such as has not existed since Colonial days." Said Walter Jones, New Jersey State Senator and Republican Party leader in Bergen County, "The very purposes of the bistate compact establishing the Port of New York Authority are in grave danger. A desire for vengeance is in the air." [33] Given these performances, one is disinclined to believe that major surrenders of existing prerogatives are close at hand.

In the less formal circles of political activity, much the same characteristics of divisiveness are on display. The business community, in various garbs, has been represented as concerned with economic development across the region. So far, however, this concern has evidenced itself principally with respect to maintaining or increasing land values in Manhattan and Newark and to urging the limited development of the Metropolitan Regional Council. The renewal projects which the private interests have sparked directly are located in areas where the forces of regeneration already exist (as with the Downtown-Lower Manhattan Association) or where matters of special institutional concern are apparent (Morningside adjacent to Columbia University or the Bloomingdale Neighborhood Conservation Project). So far as other regional problems are concerned, the failure of private concerns to provide financial support for the Metropolitan Rapid Transit Commission emphasized the difficulties which even vitally concerned interests have in mobilizing themselves to attack this issue. As for general developmental plans, even private associations dedicated to progress in government and planning find it difficult to agree. Thus, the Regional Plan Association and the City Club of New York criticize each other's analyses and reports, almost before they are published.

Other elements of diversity and insularity also underscore the difficulty of coordinate action among the political activists. Within the city, the predominant political party has more than its usual number of factions—its leadership undergoing serious attack from members claiming that racial favoritism intrudes on party councils and from those concerned with issues of party integrity and policy. The governors of the three states meet cautiously but inconclusively on transportation and other matters; to date they prefer to work separately on the resolution of the problems. And suburban party figures show little enthusiasm for closer collaboration with their neighbors if new election districts are involved. Indeed, in many matters, suburban governments go their separate ways, impervious to entreaties of party or state loyalties.

So, in November 1959, Democratic Hudson County, fearing local revenue losses, opposed Democratic Governor Meyner in his proposal to divert turnpike funds to mass transit purposes.[34] So, in January 1960, the Republican New York legislators were reported "cool" to a Republican governor's proposal to give school districts local taxing power, the first reason being their feeling that "school board members in many areas do not exhibit enough independence as taxpayers representatives, tending rather to be 'yes men' for school superintendents."[35] Except for study committees, a thesis that the existing leadership in the region stands poised for reform and reorganization, restrained only by lack of public understanding, hardly seems plausible. It is easy to see how incumbents might suffer in a major reshuffle; it is hard to see who would get ahead.

If the region's leadership shows little inclination to take giant strides, it is not likely to be pushed by the region's electorate. No massive mumblings demanding reform seem at hand. As far as one can detect, there are no insurgent elements in either party demanding "metropolitan government"; no civic associations in Long Island, Rockland, or Monmouth seeking union now with New York City. To be sure, a formal proposal for a change in governmental structure was made in 1959, coming on the heels of Governor Rockefeller's tax proposals, but it was scarcely a move toward unity. On the contrary, at that time the cry went out—and rapidly waned— for New York City to secede from the state and establish itself as a separate commonwealth.[36] Elsewhere, attitudes toward metropolitan reform appear to have paralleled those expressed in Bergen County in 1958 when a survey asking what should be done about metropolitan problems of transportation, planning, and resource development disclosed that most voters felt they were "somebody else's headache." [37] Apathy, not anxiety, seems to be the prevalent popular mood. Political change when public problems become pressing seems quite possible. But the anticipation of problems by the localities and the development of policies and structures to meet them is another matter.

It is possible, of course, that the stimulus for reform may come from political institutions at higher echelons in the American federal system. Over a period of years, the state governments may take to heart the injunction of one study commission after another that their programs and policies are inextricably intertwined with those of the local governments in the region. They may also accept the commissions' recommendations that the activities of the regional enterprises authorized by state law need to be more effectively coordinated and rationalized. Alternatively the federal government might be persuaded to apply its not inconsiderable influence in the shaping of the pattern of development within the region. If Washington adopted standards in its home loan and guaranty programs which considered the impact of new housing developments on the suburban community concerned, as well as the effect upon the homeowner and the lender, the character of residential settlement might be quite different. If Congress were to provide federal aid for mass transportation as well as for highways, the location of both homes and factories would be further affected. If renewal and development programs, and assistance in the fields of water resources and open space, were conducted according to metropolitan rather than municipal plans, the federal influence could be felt in still a more comprehensive way. In each instance, these developments might take place without so direct and obvious a challenge to the going political systems that exist within the region itself.

The prospects seem even more substantial that informal nongovernmental concern with the course of regional economic development will sharply increase. There are strong traditions in the region for private concern with metropolitan planning; for educational and philanthropic activities designed to offer alternative courses of action which are professionally prepared; and for the sounding of alarms at what appear to be untoward governmental proposals. These traditions may now trigger a rapid evolution of quasipublic, quasiprivate programs which reflect many interests but which require no formal grants of authority. These programs could move to strengthen the prospects of coordinated guidance of urban growth.

As for the probability of actions within the formal systems themselves, however, the odds seem smaller. Certainly the evidence we have just cited concerning the disinclination of the professional political leaders to move rapidly and the unconcern of the electorate should come as no surprise. For the expectations of the reformers do violence to what we know about the objectives and mode of operation of the region's political systems. In actuality, what the reformers suggest should take place is the establishment of institutions which will "ensure the region's optimum development" and "maximize the usefulness of the region's human and material resources." The goal they see as both desirable and possible for the region's government is a major and continuing concern with the shape of the region's development.

Yet the plain fact is, of course, that few inhabitants of the region, or of the nation for that matter, have ever looked to their local governments to "optimize" or "maximize" anything. On the contrary, people have regarded these units as necessary but not especially admirable service units to provide programs which did not seem supportable through private enterprise. It has never been in the region's tradition to charge local government with the responsibility for physical and economic development. The price mechanism and the marketplace are our chosen instruments for those purposes.

We seem, now, somehow concerned at the end-products issuing from the instruments on which we have relied. And, somewhat wistfully and somewhat vaguely, we think that possibly a system of human relationships neither designed nor oriented toward that purpose can be restructured to do better. We wish this restructured system, possibly, to reconsider the transportation or land-use or water-use or recreational activities that the marketplace has encouraged. We wish it to come to grips with problems in blight, obsolescence, and poverty which the marketplace has not solved. And we would prefer it to do so quickly.

Yet, to these new purposes, we endow the system with no special urgency. On the contrary, we devise ways and means—through grants-in-aid, minimal boundary changes, new sources of revenue, and new contractual relationships—for the old set of institutions and working arrangements to survive, to improve their services, and to adjust bit by bit to changing circumstances. We make sure that in extreme crises some palliative action is taken. Wherever we can, we pattern the agency organization after the very mechanism we have found defective—and then express concern when these agencies act like their ancestors. If, in any given part of the region, public service levels fall too low, or conditions of blight and obsolescence become too severe for our taste, many of us simply move out farther into the suburbs. This is in the great American pioneering tradition of abandoning settlements we have despoiled.

It is possible, of course, that even under these circumstances of ambivalence, drastic changes will occur. Leadership may forswear present power and prerogative; the public may adopt a new consciousness toward their neighbors and embrace an ideology of metropolitan citizenship. Both may seek not the tolerable environment, but the best conditions of regional growth—a New Yorker's interpretation of the *arete* of the Greek city-state.

In a discipline as uncertain and rudimentary in its techniques of prediction as political science, we do not dismiss these possibilities out of hand. We simply record that we know of no other time when a revolution took place when the existing system was solidly established and its citizens, as they understood the goals of their domestic society, content.

NOTES

1. Luther Gulick, *Metro: Changing Problems and Lines of Attack* (Washington, 1957).
2. Otto Eckstein, *Trends in Public Expenditures in the Next Decade,* Supplementary Paper of the Committee for Economic Development (New York, 1959).

3. Harry L. Severson, "The Rising Volume of Municipal Bonds," *The Daily Bond Buyer* (June 10, 1958). This article provides a summary of his analysis. Severson has prepared an extensive review and series of projections for private circulation.
4. Roland I. Robinson, "Postwar Market for State and Local Government Securities," manuscript for National Bureau of Economic Research, dated April 1957.
5. Temporary Commission on the Fiscal Affairs of State Government, *Report*, Vol. II (Albany, 1955), p. 644.
6. Commission on Governmental Operations of the City of New York, *Interim Report* (Feb. 1, 1960), p. 80.
7. City of New York, Planning Commission, *Capital Budget Message* (New York, 1957), p. 5.
8. Merrill Folsom, "Taxes in the Suburbs Heading Up as Demand for Services Keeps Increasing," *New York Times* (Oct. 1, 1959), p. 7.
9. Samuel F. Thomas, *New York City: Its Expenditure and Revenue Patterns* (mimeographed, 1958), pp. 58-59.
10. James E. Allen, Jr., Address to the Columbia University Conference on Problems of Large School Districts (mimeographed, March 17, 1959).
11. State of New Jersey, Commission on State Tax Policy, *Ninth Report* (Trenton, 1958), p. XIX.
12. Jesse Burkhead, "Metropolitan Area Budget Structures and Their Significance for Expenditures," a paper delivered at the 52nd Annual Conference of the National Tax Association, Houston, Texas, Oct. 28, 1959.
13. Eckstein, p. 9.
14. Dick Netzer, "The Outlook for Fiscal Needs and Resources of State and Local Governments," *Proceedings of the American Economic Association* (May 1958), pp. 317-327.
15. Burkhead.
16. Netzer.
17. State of New Jersey (note 11, above), p. 3.
18. These figures are from a series constructed by the New York Metropolitan Region Study from reports by the Comptroller of the State of New York and by the New Jersey Department of the Treasury, as explained in our Appendix A.
19. Burkhead.
20. On the latest New York consideration of a major tax reform see *New York Times* accounts of Governor Rockefeller's 1960 proposals, Jan. 8, 1960.
21. See note 18, above.
22. Edgar M. Hoover and Raymond Vernon, *Anatomy of a Metropolis* (Cambridge: Harvard University Press, 1959), pp. 59-60.
23. Francis Bator, *The Question of Government Spending: Public Needs vs. Private Wants* (New York, 1960).
24. See Kilpatrick and Drury in J. Frederic Dewhurst and associates, *America's Needs and Resources*, Twentieth Century Fund (New York, 1955), chap. 18.
25. U.S. Government, Special Assistant to the President for Public Works Planning, *Planning and Public Works* (Washington, 1957). See also Department of Commerce, *Survey of Construction Plans of State and Local Government* (April 4, 1955).

26. See note 18, above.
27. For an evaluation of New York City performance specifically, see Commission on Governmental Operations of the City of New York, *Interim Report* (Feb. 1, 1960).
28. See mimeographed statement by Arthur Levitt, comptroller, State of New York, "Financial Circumstances of School Districts and Implications for State Aid Policy" (Dec. 13, 1959).
29. See note 18, above.
30. Lyle Fitch, "Metropolitan Financial Problems," *The Annals of the American Academy of Political and Social Science*, 314 (November 1957), p. 73.
31. Newspaper comment on the Metropolitan Regional Council has been substantial in the last few years, and the organization publishes a periodic *Bulletin* respecting its activities. Maxwell Lehman, deputy administrator for the City of New York, whose office functions as Secretariat to the Council, and William Cassella of the National Municipal League, who has observed the Council's activities since its inception, have furnished valuable information and observations. A summary evaluation of the Council was made by the Special Committee on Metropolitan Governmental Affairs of the Regional Plan Association in its report published in the *New York Times* (Jan. 9, 1959), p. 16. See also Regional Plan Association, *The Handling of Metropolitan Problems in Selected Regions* (mimeographed, April 1958).
32. *New York Herald Tribune* (Aug. 24, 1959), p. 24.
33. *New York Times* (May 1, 1960).
34. *New York Times* (Nov. 3, 1959), p. 1.
35. *New York Times* (Jan. 8, 1960), p. 1.
36. *New York Times* (Jan. 17, 1959), p. 1.
37. *Bergen Evening Record* (Dec. 3, 1958), p. 1.

SUGGESTED READINGS

Andrews, Richard B., *Urban Growth and Development*. New York: Simmons-Boardman, 1962.

Bebout, John E., and Biedemeier, Harry C., "American Cities As Social Systems," *Journal of the American Institute of Planners*, Vol. XXIX, No. 2, May 1963, 64-76.

Bollens, John C., ed., *Exploring the Metropolitan Community*. Berkeley and Los Angeles: University of California Press, 1961.

————, *Special District Governments in the United States*. Berkeley and Los Angeles: University of California Press, 1957.

Brazer, Harvey E., "The Role of Major Metropolitan Centers in State and Local Finance," *American Economic Review*, Vol. 48, May 1958, 305-316.

Churchill, Henry S., *The City Is the People*. New York: Reynal and Hitchcock, 1945.

Committee for Economic Development, *The "Little" Economies: Problems of U.S. Area Development*. New York, May 1958.

Connery, Robert H., and Leach, Richard H., *The Federal Government and Metropolitan Areas*. Cambridge: Harvard University Press, 1960.

Fiser, Webb S., *Mastery of the Metropolis*. Englewood Cliffs, N.J.: Prentice-Hall, 1962. A Spectrum Book, S-28.

Fortune editors, *The Exploding Metropolis*. Garden City, N.Y.: Doubleday, 1957-58.

Futterman, Robert, *The Future of Our Cities*. Garden City, N.Y.: Doubleday, 1961.

Geen, Elizabeth; Lowe, I. R.; and Walker, K., *Man and the Modern City*. Pittsburgh: University of Pittsburgh Press, 1963.

Gordon, Mitchell, *Sick Cities*. New York: Macmillan, 1963.

Gottman, Jean, *Megapolis: the Urbanized Northeastern Seaboard of the United States*. New York: Twentieth Century Fund, 1961.

Greer, Scott, *The Emerging City, Myth and Reality*. New York: Free Press of Glencoe, 1962.

————, *Metropolitics: A Study of Political Culture*. New York: Wiley, 1963.

Gulick, Luther, *Changing Problems and Lines of Attack*. Washington, D.C.: Governmental Affairs Institute, 1957.

————, *The Metropolitan Problem and American Ideas*. New York: Knopf, 1962.

Higbee, Edward C., *The Squeeze: Cities Without Space*. New York: William Morrow, 1960.

Hoover, Edgar M., and Vernon, Raymond, *Anatomy of A Metropolis*. Cambridge: Harvard University Press, 1959.

Jacobs, Jane, *The Death and Life of Great American Cities*. New York: Random House, 1961.

Lichfield, Nathaniel, *Cost Benefit Analysis in Urban Redevelopment*. Real Estate Research Program Report No. 20, Institute of Business and Economic Research, University of California. Berkeley: University of California Press, 1962.

Lynd, Staughton, "Urban Renewal—For Whom?" *Commentary*, Vol. 31, January 1961, 34-45, and March 1961, 255-256.

Margolis, Julius, "Municipal Fiscal Structure in a Metropolitan Region," *Journal of Political Economy*, Vol. 65, June 1957, 225-236.

"Metropolis in Ferment," *The Annals of the American Academy of Political and Social Science*, Vol. 314, November 1957 (entire issue).

Nixon, John H., "Transportation in the Central City," *Planning, 1963* (Proceedings of the American Society of Planning Officials National Planning Conference, Seattle, Washington, May 5-9, 1963), 140-147.

Owen, Wilfred, *The Metropolitan Transportation Problem*. Washington, D.C.: Brookings, 1956.

Perloff, Harvey S.; Dunn, Edgar S., Jr.; Lampard, Eric E.; and Muth, Richard F.; *Regions, Resources and Economic Growth*. (For Resources For the Future, Inc.) Baltimore: Johns Hopkins Press, 1960.

Pittsburgh Regional Planning Association (Economic Study of the Pittsburgh Region), Vol. I, *Region in Transition;* Vol. II, *Portrait of a Region;* Vol. III, *Region with a Future*. Pittsburgh: University of Pittsburgh Press, 1963.

"Planning the City's Center," *Journal of the American Institute of Planners*, Vol. XXVII, No. 1, February 1961 (entire issue).

Richey, Elinor, "Splitsville, U.S.A.: An Ironic Tale of Urban Renewal and Racial Segregation," *The Reporter,* Vol. 28, No. 11, May 23, 1963, 35-38.

Sengstock, Frank S., *Extraterritorial Powers in the Metropolitan Area.* Ann Arbor: University of Michigan Law School, 1962.

Southeastern Michigan Metropolitan Community Research Corporation, *Our Metropolitan Community: What Goods and Guidelines.* Frank M. Kubata, ed., Detroit, 1963.

"Transportation Renaissance," *The Annals of the American Academy of Political and Social Science.* Vol. 345, January 1963 (entire issue).

U. S. Advisory Commission on Intergovernmental Relations, *Alternative Approaches to Intergovernmental Reorganization in Metropolitan Areas.* Washington, D.C.: Government Printing Office, 1962.

U. S. Advisory Commission on Intergovernmental Relations, *Governmental Structure, Organization and Planning in Metropolitan Areas.* Washington, D.C.: Government Printing Office, 1961.

U. S. Advisory Commission on Intergovernmental Relations, *Intergovernmental Responsibilities for Mass Transportation Facilities and Services in Metropolitan Areas.* Washington, D.C.: Government Printing Office, 1961.

Vernon, Raymond, *The Changing Economic Function of the Central City.* New York: Committee for Economic Development, 1959.

Weaver, Robert C., "Class, Race and Urban Renewal," *Land Economics,* Vol. 36, No. 3, August 1960, 235-251.

Wheaton, William L. C., and Schussheim, Morton J., *Cost of Municipal Services in Residential Areas.* Washington, D.C.: U. S. Department of Commerce, 1955.

Wingo, Lowden, Jr., *Transportation and Urban Land.* Washington, D.C.: Resources For the Future, Inc., 1961.

Wood, Robert C., *1400 Governments.* Cambridge: Harvard University Press, 1961.

———, *Metropolis Against Itself.* New York: Committee for Economic Development, 1959.

ALSO IN THE MODERN ECONOMIC ISSUES SERIES